Dog Days and Dragonflies

By
Chrissie Anderson Peters

CAP Publishing
Bristol, TN

Dog Days and Dragonflies (Revised Edition)

CAP Publishing
284 Midway Dr.
Bristol, TN 37620
www.ChrissieAndersonPeters.com
Phone: 423.646.8659

This book is comprised of stories that are both fictional and
nonfictional in nature, the nonfictional parts based on memories
of the author. These memories may differ from the memories of
others involved, but are set down as they are for the sake of art
and telling specific stories. No malicious or falsified comments
are intended by the author.

Book cover designed by Beth Jorgensen; book cover art
copyright © 2012 Beth Jorgensen.

Printed in the United States of America

ISBN-13: 978-0985257408
ISBN-10: 0985257407

Dog Days and Dragonflies

By
Chrissie Anderson Peters

25 April 2013

To Gina~
So awesome to see you again and
catch up! Enjoy these stories and
poems and may all of your wild bird
wishes come true!

Chrissie Anderson Peters

CAP Publishing

To my amazing husband, Russ: thanks for your never-ending support, for your unwavering/unconditional love, and for your gift of believing in my dreams, even when I wasn't sure that they were attainable.

To my family and friends: you have made me who I am and have shaped the stories in this book, as well as my imagination and experiences. Mom, I love you very much!

To my "writing family" at Lincoln Memorial University's Mountain Heritage Literary Festival and at the Hindman Settlement School's Appalachian Writers Workshop: you never made it a competition or chore, but instead accepted me, encouraged me, guided me, loved me, and celebrated me, and then you helped me make sure the words were right.

And with thanks to my great-grandmother, Daisy Irene Hash Vance (30 July 1910 – 27 May 1978), whose smile and spirit are with me always; whose "list" still guides me after nearly 35 years; and whose love not only covered her children, but also her grandchildren and great-grandchildren; I know that you are my most devoted muse and help me find strength in stories of family and kin.

~ CAP
31 May 2012

Advance Praise for *Dog Days and Dragonflies*

"*Dog Days and Dragonflies* is Chrissie Anderson Peters' tribute to the people who made her, especially her mother and her grandparents. She writes for her life in these personal essays, short stories, and poems, detailing a childhood world of both hardship and tragedy and also love and contentment. Many in these stories and poems are maimed in some way, the walking wounded, but they showed her how to not only survive, but thrive. This book is the story of all kinds of salvation, how all the old verities – family, church, community, work, and nature – are all finally the only important things. *Dog Days and Dragonflies* reminds us to be always hopeful and to wait for our 'red bird wishes' to come true." ~ Rita Sims Quillen, author of *Her Secret Dream* and a finalist for Poet Laureate of Virginia for 2012

~ ~ ~

"If you're looking for brave vision in a new voice, *Dog Days and Dragonflies* is the book for you. Chrissie Anderson Peters' stories of friendship, hardship, family love and betrayal will stay with you long past the last page." ~ George Ella Lyon, author of *She Let Herself Go*

~ ~ ~

"Imagine learning to drive an old pickup in a hayfield, your grandpa teaching you. But instead of riding beside you, Grandpa walks in front of you. Which of those three pedals do you press to stop? That tension and humor will pull you along through Chrissie Anderson Peters' *Dog Days and Dragonflies*." ~ Jim Minick, author of *The Blueberry Years*

~ ~ ~

"These stories and poems by Chrissie Anderson Peters are a real delight, full of nostalgia but also a hard reality of strong, tough women and broken men. And the facts are wonderfully vivid, from the smell of crayons in a box to the grandmother who holds a lit match to let a little girl blow it out." ~ James Whorton, Jr., author of *Angela Sloan*

~ ~ ~

"Chrissie Anderson Peters takes us into the complicated, dark, and beautiful heart of contemporary Appalachia with these intriguing stories, essays, and poems." ~ Silas House, author of *Same Sun Here* and *Parchment of Leaves*

Preface

    Dog Days and Dragonflies has come to exist in this incarnation through several drafts and over the course of about six years with the exception of one poem from the late 1980's. When I started the journey that would become what is contained within these pages, I thought that it would be a quick turn-around kind of project. In fact, when I sent out Christmas cards in December 2011, I told people to stay tuned for details for purchasing the book in early 2012. I thought that it would be quick because I envisioned the project to be comprised of a collection of stories and poems that have been published in smaller regional journals and literary magazines since 2006. How hard could it be to self-publish a collection of such materials?

    But then I realized that I didn't want to just rush through this project. What I wanted to do was to publish a collection that would show my interests, my passions, and also my growth in the past six years as a writer. I wanted to publish a collection that would interest others, not just my immediate family and closest friends. I wanted to publish a collection that I could – and would – be proud of.

    Even though I have learned many things about good writing in the past few years, I didn't want to wait to try to get a contract for the collection of stories and poems with a traditional publisher. Traditional publishing, *if* an author is able to score a contract for his/her book, usually takes at least a couple of years. In all honesty, I never felt like I had that much time to wait for this project. This collection is for me, but it's for so many other people, too – including my three living grandparents: Arthur James Little (who will be 88 in November 2012) and Dorothy Irene Vance Little (who will be 82 in August 2012); and James Virgil Anderson (who turned 100 in March 2012). But in the process of trying to make this collection ready, I lost others near and dear to me (especially Jeffrey Weaver, a cousin many times over) and was reminded that none of us has the promise of tomorrow. Life is short and I felt like I needed to put this collection in the hands of so many who have helped to make me who I am before any more time passed.

    I believed from the beginning inklings of this collection coming together that self-publishing would be the best way to proceed with the project; after Peggy DeKay's one-day workshop at the Carnegie Center in Lexington, Kentucky, in February 2012, I was *certain* that it was the best way to go. Even with a contract and a traditional publisher, most authors are left to their own devices for the tasks of marketing and promotion of the written work. So, I was encouraged once again to look at the advantages of self-publishing: either way, I would be doing the bulk of my own marketing and promotion; with self-publishing, I get to keep the profits that a traditional publisher would take for "publishing" my material. I wasn't a math major, but *even I* understand *that* math.

Almost anything that I write is based in some way or another in real-life experience, whether mine or someone else's. I do not label the stories in this collection in such a way to alert the reader as to which ones specifically are fiction and which are nonfiction. My primary goal is to present a story that people can read and enjoy, relate to, etc. Those who are familiar with the people and places of my life may well be able to identify people by name – others may think that they know, but I'll never tell! The people who *are not* fictitious folks are usually identified by name. But often, I change the names in attempts of not offending others who might have been involved with the story in some way. Having said all of that, however, I also sometimes plug familiar people, places, and/or situations into storylines I have imagined in order to make a story feel less "fictional" than it actually is.

My mother has repeatedly told me, "Don't write anything bad about us!" As I've tried to explain to her on numerous occasions, I do not write anything with the intent of hurting anyone's feelings or disrupting their affections. I love my family, both my Littles and my Andersons. When I write about things that happened in the past, I have done so with the purpose of exploring it retrospectively, hoping to make sense out of it as an adult that I was not always able to accomplish as a child. Rather than becoming angry or taking offense in any way, I hope that my readers who think that they see themselves in the stories in this collection will try to see the situation as it is being presented, not as an attack against them in any way. In other words, don't take anything personally. If you feel guilty, it's much more likely that it is your conscience convicting you than my words or stories.

The people, places, and stories presented in *Dog Days and Dragonflies* are, by and large, stories of my life. From my perspective.

And with that claim, I will also admit that memories are not always how we perceive them. That is part of the "trick" of writing creative nonfiction or memoir. I have constructed and herein present these stories and poems how I have *perceived* the stories within and behind them. Again, any differences between my perception of reality and others' perceptions of reality is personal and nothing by which I mean any malice.

As a teenager, I despised being from Tazewell, Virginia; I hated being from Appalachia. I tried my best to lose my accent; I swore I would never go back to Tazewell after college. However, I am blessed that God insisted otherwise! He took me back to Tazewell, not to put me in a teaching position, which was what my college work was to have prepared me to do, but to help me gain a sense of appreciation for my hometown, for my family, for who I was and would continue to be. At the time, I remember feeling like a failure for ending up back in Tazewell. But two years later, when I left Tazewell for a job in Roanoke, I was glad for the opportunity to learn to love what I had taken for granted or even denied as part of myself for my first twenty-one years of life.

Today, I couldn't be prouder to be who I am: an Appalachian; a Tazewellian; a descendant of numerous families based in Southwest Virginia and Western North Carolina for well over 200 years – Little, Vance, Anderson, Parks, and a slew of other surnames known for their independence and survival over the years. I am thankful for the gifts that God has given me and am glad that, despite a hiatus of about a decade or so, I am once again writing for my life. I hope that you will read these stories and poems and see the strength of character and survival skills under which I was raised. I hope that you will enjoy the stories that have come from this journey so far.

~ Chrissie Anderson Peters
4 June 2012, Bristol, TN

Acknowledgments

This collection of stories and poems did not just spring forth from my head and my heart. They were nurtured and grown with the love, support, and encouragement of many kind souls. I am almost afraid to begin naming names, for fear of forgetting someone. Yet, I feel compelled to thank so many personally for all that they have done to see this project become a reality.

First of all, I wish to thank God for His abundant gifts and never-ending compassion. During the times that I didn't think that I could make it, He always provided a way.

To my husband, Russell Peters, I can't begin to thank you enough for all of your love, your encouragement, and support. Even when others who were close to me thought I was crazy or mean-spirited to put down these stories and poems as I have, you stood by me. You told me to keep reaching, keep writing, and you never made me feel guilty for hovering over a computer screen when there were certainly other things that we could be doing together. More than ten years into this amazing marriage we have built and nurtured together, I still find myself wondering how we have done it, but so incredibly glad that we have kept at it day by day. With all that I am and ever shall be....

To my family, both my mother's side (the Littles and the Vances) and my father's side (the Andersons and the Parkses), I thank you for loving me, for teaching me how to make my own way in this world, and also for sharing generations of stories and tall tales that became the colorful fabric of the backdrop of my existence. Thanks for amazing family reunions and for teaching me about those who came before me. And to my cousins – especially Melenia Edwards Stryker, Melissa Little South, Jesse "Andy" Little, and Adam Little – I am so glad that we had the opportunity to grow up together and that you are such important characters to my life story. To Sarah Williams, Jessica Williams, Kedric Edwards, Missy Anderson Barnes, and Megan Krum, I love each of you and don't want you to think that I've forgotten you!

To my "genealogy" family, I cannot thank you enough for leading me to other family stories that have helped me learn more about my family lines. Particularly to the fine folks at NewRiverNotes.com and both the Grayson County, Virginia Heritage Foundation and the Tazewell County [Virginia] Historical Society, thanks for putting up with my many questions once I started researching our numerous and tangled family lines on my own, too. Someday, we'll figure out all those brick walls, I hope, and get to the stories behind all of these fascinating people from whom we descend.

To my many school friends back home in Tazewell, thanks for so many wonderful times and memories. Thanks for always believing that I had at least one book in me. I hope to get a few more out of my system before all is said and done. I especially want to thank Becky Baldwin Cisco for the renewal on our decades-old friendship and all of her encouragement as this project came together.

Anyone who knows me knows that church was an important part of my childhood and growing-up years, even though we changed churches frequently. So, to my friends and family from the following churches, I wish to say thank you for prayers and love, and for serving as role models for so long: Yost Chapel Freewill Baptist Church, Central Church of Christ, Tazewell First Assembly of God, Dailey's Chapel, and Adria Advent Christian Church.

To my amazing college friends from Emory & Henry, more thanks and appreciation. You are the folks I credit with shaping who I've become in many ways. To the Sisters of Pi Sigma Kappa, and the Brothers of Sigma Alpha Kappa, a special thanks for showing me how wonderful "families" can be, even when they disagree and don't always get along well; I still marvel at who we have all become and am so proud to this day that I ran up the hill to the Pi Kapp Tree. I wish to acknowledge a few of you by name – just because you've always been there and I suspect that you always will be, which is an immense comfort to me: Traci Hurt Brandon, Myrica Cook, Anna Buchanan Martin, Julie Thompson Anderson, and my "Awesome Big" ("Lynne-Lynne-Lover-of-Men; I said it once – I'll say it again") Lynne Bishop. Some of you have been reading, editing, and giving me feedback for more than two decades – thanks so much for those gifts of time and talent! Also, to Buffy Milhorne, Malissa Brown Trent, Beth Andis Fairbanks, Laurie Stacy Adams, Liz Lambert Whitlock, Mary Beth Carter Greer, Penny Lane Stevens, Lisa McDowell, Karen Kroeker, Duncan Granger, Jarrett Potts, Jimmy Self, Jason Lipscomb, Dave Jackson, Erick Long, Brad Wise, Doug Dalton, and the other extraordinary "purple people" at E&H, thanks for more good times and amazing hugs than I could possibly ever remember. And to Jenny

Poston Bishop and Tamara Davis – our Greek letters were different, but you are Sisters of my heart!

To my beloved co-"Pioneers" from the UT School of Information Sciences first online cohort, thanks for making what was sometimes a stressful situation a lot more tolerable and fun. I miss you guys and am also proud of how we have all added to our career field. Librarians ROCK!

I also owe a great debt to several educators who, over the years, provided examples of how to live and learn and served as some of the most phenomenal role models I could have ever been blessed to have known. This list of individuals includes Helen Bourne, Thomas George, Betty Yates, Waverly Moss, Martha Chaffins, Tom Chaffins, Susan Whittaker, Leon Yost, Marti Bowen, Carol Hart, Tammi Meade Ferguson, Nancy Wallace, Mary Thomason, Terri Mitchell, Fred Dean, Iva Dean, Jerry Cromer, Prof. Alan Pickrell, Dr. John Lang, Dr. Kathleen Chamberlain, Dr. Felicia Mitchell, Dr. Robin Reid, Dr. Jinx Watson, Dr. Bill Robinson, and Dr. Carol Tenopir.

During the nearly twenty years that I have worked in libraries, I have also come to know some really amazing people who gave me the opportunity to prove myself in the field. Beginning in Tazewell County with Laurie Surface Roberts, who gave me my first library position, and Sarah Lineberry, who taught me how to be a children's librarian, I have been blessed with lots of great professional experiences. Also in Tazewell County, I wish to publically decree that I would have lost my mind had it not been for Sharee Hale Bowman and Sandy Mosolgo – I love you both so much! I also want to thank Steve Vest (Blue Ridge Library in Botetourt County), who may well be the coolest boss I ever had; I really appreciate all of the things that you taught me. To Steve Preston and the folks at Bedford Public Library, thank you for the opportunity to show you what I could do, even though I did not have a Masters degree. To my friends just up the road at Bristol Public Library, thank you for giving me my professional start in what has become my home (Bristol); especially to Jeanne Powers, who is still the litmus test I use for anyone claiming to be a Reference Librarian and to Michelle Page, who will never grow up – for which I am glad! I am also indebted to Theresa McMahan at Sullivan County Public Library and Vickie Combs at Barnes & Noble in Johnson City for their encouragement, support, and inspiration.

I would be remiss if I didn't mention my colleagues at Northeast State Community College, my workplace for more than a decade now. Virginia Salmon, Annis Evans, John Grubb, Chris Demas, Michelle Wyatt, Dawn Kraft, Amy Hopkins, Jason Penwell, Cindy Robins McMurray, and Duncan Parsons – you have given me room to experiment and room to grow, and for this, I am greatly indebted. Aside from my co-workers in the library, though, I am appreciative and thankful for many other instructors at Northeast State. I won't even try to name all of you – please don't be upset with me for that. I will, however, give props where they are due: to Tamara Baxter and Gretchen McCroskey, without your Creative Writing classes, I'm not sure where I would be right now. The two of you have nurtured the "adult" me and I am so thankful for both of you!

In the past couple of years, I have discovered two havens of writing talent and instruction that I would surely be lost without. I owe more debts of personal and "writing" gratitude than I could ever possibly pay to the fine folks who head up the Mountain Heritage Literary Festival at Lincoln Memorial University in Harrogate, TN: Silas House and Denton Loving, co-founders of this festival have created an event that is more than that – it is a living organism, one filled with talent and nurturing writers – and continues to grow in scope, in depth, and in popularity, thanks to the hard work put forth by Denton Loving and LMU's current Writer-in-Residence, Darnell Arnoult. Many thanks to my instructors at the MHLF over the past three summers – Anne Shelby, Jason Howard, Pamela Duncan, and Joseph Bathanti. For thirty-five years now, along the banks of the forks of Troublesome Creek, in Knott County, Kentucky, a group of people anointed with the gift of words have gathered at the Hindman Settlement School's Appalachian Writers Workshop. I have been blessed to be part of this awe-inspiring community for three summers now and cannot begin to express how much that honor means to me. Here, I have sat with instructors of the written word including Crystal Wilkinson, Jim Minick, and George Ella Lyon and have been in lectures delivered by Robert Morgan and Lee Smith. I have shared the communion of words with current Appalachian powerhouses such as Silas House, Amy Greene, and many others. And all of them have taught me something time and time again: we're all part of the same big quilt and have our own place in this family of writers.

Another emphatic "thanks" goes to the members of the Poetry Society of Tennessee – Northeast Chapter for their constant encouragement, too. Even though I'm usually too tired or lazy to get out of bed on Saturday mornings once a month for their meetings, they continue to embrace me. That is the mark of good people! And to the members of the Boone Tree Library Association, I express great appreciation for a decade of programs and people celebrating libraries, learning, and book-loving in Northeast Tennessee!

With regards to this particular project, I need to thank numerous folks. To Virginia Salmon, my primary reader and "editor," I appreciate all of your comments, questions, and suggestions: *Dog Days and Dragonflies* is an immensely better book because of your watchful eye and editorial talents. I would also like to thank my five author-friends who provided blurbs and advance praise for the book: Silas House, George Ella Lyon, Jim Minick, Rita Quillen, and James Whorton, Jr. Your words about my words uplifted me and will hopefully help others see what this book is all about!

To all of the friends/fans of our Facebook page (www.facebook.com/pages/Dog-Days-and-Dragonflies/370301479680097), a very special thanks! Without your interest and without you helping to spread the word about this project, the road would have been lonely and less fun, indeed.

What would any book be without a cover? A book, still, but not so interesting on the outside, for certain. Since God did not give me "pictures" to go with my words, I launched a contest through the Facebook page to get a cover for Dog *Days and Dragonflies*. I posted the announcement via my FB page and know that numerous others did the same. The result was four beautiful entries that each spoke to me in some way. Everyone who had "liked" the book's page got one vote to vote for his/her favorite entry. The top three vote-getters moved on to a panel, who then selected the book cover contest winner. Many thanks to my panelists who did a fantastic job, with a quick turn-around: Jay McCoy, who reads more than anyone I know and therefore has examined a lot of book covers; Dr. Bill Robinson, retired from the University of Tennessee's School of Information Sciences, who taught a course on book design which taught me lots when I took it during my Masters degree pursuit; and Staci Schoenfeld, a current graduate student at Southern Illinois University in Carbondale, who also reads diversely and knows a great book cover when she sees it. The book cover contest winner, Beth Jorgensen, currently resides in Arizona, but also hails from Tazewell County, Virginia. In fact, Beth and I are second cousins, and both grew up in Baptist Valley (she on the Richlands end and I on the Tazewell end), but have never met! Read more about this talented artist and her work at the end of the book, on the "About the Author/About the Book Cover Artist" page. I also wish to give a shout-out to my friend Charity Peery Higgins of Shooting Star Photography in Johnson City, TN. Charity did the "author" photographs for me and wouldn't't hear of me paying for them; so if you like the photo on the back of the book and live locally, check out their website (http://www.higginsshootingstar.com) and send some business their way! (As a side note, Charity's Peerys also hail from Tazewell County – so many "small-world" connections for all of us!)

I need to thank my closest "writing family" members. These are the folks who read stuff for me from a distance all year long and who share contest information and publication opportunities with me year-round. They are the ones who tell me when something isn't nearly as good as I think/hope it is, but also the ones who point out so many positives that I often overlook in my own writing; they encourage and sustain me in so many ways, every day. These are my "brothers and sisters of the written word" and they are above all worth! To Elizabeth Glass, Denton Loving, Jay McCoy, Staci Schoenfeld, Savannah Sipple, and Nikaya Smith, thanks for always being there and for never steering me wrong! And one final word of thanks to Denton Loving, who flat-out told me to find a better title for this book than *So Far* and lit up when I mentioned the possibility of *Dog Days and Dragonflies*; based on feedback and comments I've gotten so far, you were (as usual) absolutely correct!

And to Misty Buchanan Dishner, my feline children's godmother , thanks for all you do, both with the cats and to help me out and support me in my writing. You are a true treasure!

If I have overlooked anyone, I promise it was not intentionally. So many people over the years have contributed so much to my writing and I sincerely do appreciate every single one of you!

~ Chrissie Anderson Peters

I would be remiss if I did not take the time to thank and acknowledge the various publications/competitions which have previously published my work.

The following pieces have appeared in *Echoes & Images*, the Northeast State Community College Student Literary and Visual Arts Magazine, an annual publication of Northeast State Community College in Blountville, Tennessee: "I Didn't Get Anything of Granny's" (Vol. 16, Spring 2006), "Road Trip Graffiti" (Vol. 16, Spring 2006), "Speaking in Tongues" (Vol. 19, Spring 2009), "Hillbillies" (Vol. 19, Spring 2009), "The Funeral" (Vol. 19, Spring 2009), "Something Stupid" (Vol. 19, Spring 2009), "Ice Cream Truck" (Vol. 20, Spring 2010), "A Day With Granny [Poem]" (Vol. 20, Spring 2010), "Retail Hell" (Vol. 20, Spring 2010), and "Mrs. Betty Jo Yates" (Vol. 20, Spring 2010).

The following pieces have appeared in *Clinch Mountain Review*, a literary review of Southwest Virginia: "Childhood Sunday Mornings" (2010), "Crying" (2010), "The Saddest Obituary" (2010), "Winter Rains" (2010); "Leah's Lullaby" (2011); "Wrapping Meat" (2011); and "The Manor" (2011).

The poem "Dog Days and Dragonflies" appeared in the 2011 issue of *The Howl*, a literary and art review of Virginia Highlands Community College.

The poem "Freedom" appeared in Volume 14 of *Pine Mountain Sand & Gravel*. "Come Home, My Cousins, Come Home" appeared in Volume 15.

The poem "Priest of Nothing" tied for first place in the high school category of the 1989 writing competition for the Chautauqua Festival based in Wytheville, Virginia.

"Corey's Quarry" received 2nd place in the 2011 Watauga Chapter of the League of National PenWomen Contest.

"Learning to Drive" received 2nd place in Nonfiction for the 2011 contest of the Tennessee Mountain Writers.

The poem "Crazy" placed 2nd in a monthly contest with the Poetry Society of Tennessee and 3rd Honorable Mention in the 2012 Joe Pendeleton Campbell Memorial contest (Poetry Society of Virginia).

Stories: Fact and Fiction

Poetry: Lyrics and Verse

Part I

Stories: Fact and Fiction

A Day With Granny

"Come on, Chrissy," Papaw said, holding up my heavy winter coat. "Time to go to Granny's!"

It was a normal day in 1975. Nearly every day of my pre-school life was spent at my great-grandparents' house in Baptist Valley. Mom and I lived with my grandparents, just a short five-minute-drive away.

I put my arms in and Papaw zipped me up. I raced out to the car. Mamaw was already sitting there, wearing her plastic rain bonnet to keep snow off of her hair because she'd gotten it fixed the afternoon before. Papaw put me in the back seat and closed the door. There were no seat belts or car seats back then, and as Papaw started the car, I scooted over to the middle of the backseat, resting my chin on the seat in front of me, excited to go to Granny's and thrilled to see snow falling in fuzzy, fat flakes.

The roads were covered with snow. Even though Papaw drove more slowly than usual, Mamaw repeatedly admonished, "Lord! Slow down! You're gonna get us killed!" I could see him roll his eyes through the rearview mirror and tried not to giggle.

Papaw carried me so I wouldn't track snow in. The instant that my feet touched the floor, I ran down the hall calling, "Granny! I'm here!"

Granny had just pulled herself around to the front side of the bed. She slept in the back, where there was little room to get in or out, even for me. It was really hard for a grown-up and next-to-impossible for Granny because she didn't have one of her legs. She looked up and motioned me into the bedroom that doubled as a sort of living room. I ran in and hugged her tightly as she gathered me up in her arms, still sitting on the edge of the bed. "Good morning," she smiled and kissed me.

"Hi, Granny! Where's Granddaddy?"

"I reckon he must be outside somewhere," she sighed.

"Granny, it's snowing! Did you see the snow yet?" I ran over to the window and lifted up the shade to try to show her.

"I'll see it well enough in a few minutes," she answered. "Hand Granny her leg there, will you, baby?"

Her prosthetic leg rested at the foot of the bed, near the window I stood beside. It was heavy. There was a plain black shoe at the bottom of it, as well as pantyhose pulled up to the knee of it, where it would fit onto where her real leg left off. I dragged it over to the side of the bed and finally got it to her as Mamaw entered the room and shook melted snow off of her rain bonnet. "Mommy, I was on my way in! Don't make Chrissy bring you that! She don't understand and it might scare her!"

She was wrong. Granny was my buddy. We did everything together. I didn't mind helping her at all. I might not have understood why she had a fake leg, but it didn't scare me.

Granny mumbled under her breath, so that only she and I could hear. "I ain't gonna do nothing to scare this baby, am I?" I smiled, shook my head, and hugged her again, patting the soft, cool, wrinkled skin of her cheeks.

Mamaw made me move to give Granny room. I sat in Granddaddy's swivel lounger and watched as she pulled, tugged, and fixed the leg into place. Still sitting on the bed, she reached across to Granddaddy's foot trunk beside the

TV and pulled her pink button-up sweater on. Then she hoisted herself up, taking a few seconds to get her balance before making her way into the kitchen.

I ran in front of her. "Look, Granny! Look at the snow!" I pointed excitedly, running to the kitchen window beside her Hoosier cupboard, where I played store every day.

She shook her head in disdain, "Yes, I see. I've gotta go out in it to get some coal."

But just as she said it, Papaw came in the back door with the coal bucket full. "Daisy, watch back! I've got this. I'm gonna go back out to the coal house and get some more to keep you and Jess through the night and into tomorrow in case it keeps snowing." She patted him heartily on the back and started into the rest of her daily routine.

She tied an apron around her waist before sitting down at her end of the kitchen table, taking a can of Prince Albert tobacco and some rolling papers from the apron pocket. With shaky fingers, she pulled a single rolling paper from the pack with the Indian chief's head on it. Raising her finger to her mouth, she pulled it across her tongue, then drew it along the upper edge of the rolling paper. Next, she carefully opened the can of Prince Albert and lifted it to pour a thin line of tobacco into the crease of the rolling paper. With both hands now involved in the cigarette-rolling process, she used her wrist and elbow to close the lid on old Prince Albert and continued to roll the cigarette, tamping down the tobacco and pressing it back in the ends with one fingertip when it tried to escape as she rolled it. She wet her finger one more time to ascertain that the tobacco was perfectly contained within the paper, then smiled as she appraised the end result. Her eyes blinked – a nervous tic, perhaps, or maybe from allergies or something else. She lit the little cigarette, then held out the match so I could blow it out. I giggled and she hugged me again.

"Mommy, you shouldn't smoke right in her face like that," Mamaw interjected as she took re-heated biscuits from the oven and placed them on the table. Granny grumbled something and released me from her arms, shaking her head.

Once she had smoked her cigarette, she pulled up from the kitchen table and steadied herself as she began walking around the kitchen to get dinner started. Lest there be any confusion, *dinner* was Granddaddy's noon-time meal; *supper* was his evening meal. As Granny busied herself at the cook stove, I set up my play store by opening the door to the Hoosier cupboard, propping it open with one of the kitchen chairs. "Baby, Granny needs some Crisco."

I reached into the cupboard and lifted the three-pound can of Crisco shortening with Loretta Lynn's picture on the side. "That'll be five cents," I informed her. And she plucked pretend money from her apron pocket and handed it to me with a grin and a wink.

I watched as she plopped a big spoonful of shortening into her cast iron skillet. While it was melting and heating, she prepared a bowl of cornbread mix – cornmeal, buttermilk, sweet milk, flour, and just a pinch of salt. When the grease was just the right temperature, she spooned the cornbread mixture into the cast iron skillet and it hissed a pleasant hiss, a hiss that promised something warm and delicious would soon be delivered. I often mimicked many of her actions in my own little pretend kitchen in my play store. Mamaw helped her peel potatoes and fry up some Treet meat in another skillet. The kitchen smelled of all things good and right.

Mamaw went to the back door, calling loudly for Papaw and Granddaddy. "Come eat, y'all! Dinner's on the table." This was a slight exaggeration, as Granny never put things on the table until Granddaddy could be seen coming through the gate separating the backyard from the fields. Once he got that far, she began taking things off the stove, putting them on pot holders on the table. By then, he was usually coming in the back door, stomping his boots, taking off his gray Stetson fedora. He would walk slowly from the kitchen into their bedroom, then into the bathroom, where he closed the door behind him. A few minutes later, he would emerge smelling like Life Buoy soap. Meanwhile, Granny would make him a plate and have it ready, dish towel on one side of his plate and silverware on the other side. Only after he had sat down to eat would she turn back to the stove to get her own plate. Granddaddy solemnly said the grace, "Dear Father, bless this food to the nourishment of our bodies to make us strong and able. Amen."

After dinner, Mamaw and Granny gathered up the dishes, took them to the sink, and washed them. When the dishes were put away, we proceeded to the bedroom and turned on the television set. It was my favorite time of day: time for Granny's "stories."

Before the theme for *The Doctors* was finished, she had another cigarette rolled and had leaned back in her swivel lounger, taking leave of her actual surroundings. By the time *Days of Our Lives* had come and gone, she had been transported completely to *Another World*. She talked to the people on her stories as though they were right there in the room with us. She laughed with them, told them off, cussed at them, and every now and then, wiped a tear from her eye when things weren't going well for them. She fretted over feuding couples and got so agitated when the characters didn't heed her advice. "I TOLD you not to fool with that girl, that she'd just get you into trouble and now LOOK! I told you NOT to fool with her, boy!"

When the stories went off, we went back to the kitchen. Today, Mamaw wanted to dust the front parlor, so Granny told her to go ahead. Granny and I sat together talking about the snow. Her watery blue eyes looked as clouded as the skies overhead as she set to looking for a red bird. "Help me look, baby. Let's find us a red bird and make a wish." Our eyes scanned the great outdoors to find a red bird.

Then we saw one and Granny gathered me near and whispered, "Quiet now, say the poem and make a wish, then blow it a kiss before it flies away." Red birds don't typically light for long, so it was rare to complete this whole ritual before one flew away.

"Red bird, carry my wish with you; red bird, make my wish come true!" We both made our wishes, blew it a kiss, and I marveled that it had stayed put for so long.

"What did you wish for, Granny?"

"Oh, you can't tell your wish. If you do, it won't come true." She kissed my cheek as she wiped at her eyes.

By late afternoon it was dark outside already, but I could see Granny in the doorway as we piled into the car. I climbed into the car's back window to wave at her until the house was completely out of sight. Tomorrow would be much the same thing, and the day after that, too. I never tired of it.

More than thirty years later, those cornbread-flavored days of playing store and watching Granny's stories, observing the rituals of cigarette-rolling and putting on her leg every morning still play in my mind like they happened this very morning. I know Granny's real "stories" now, though – how Granddaddy shot her in the leg when she was eight months pregnant with their fourth child; how hard she worked to keep peace in that farmhouse despite Granddaddy's impossible temper; how much pride she took in taking care of others, rather than focusing on her own needs and wishes. Wishes… I realize now that those red birds may have been the only creatures she ever shared her true thoughts with, and each one carried more than snowflakes on its wings on snowy winter days.

Mrs. Betty Jo Yates

It was the only time I can recall school starting back on a Monday, rather than on a Thursday. I never understood the logic of starting school on a Thursday, quite honestly: you got started back into a routine, then boom! It was the weekend and you got thrown off all over again. But fifth grade was not to be this way; we would go an entire week before the blessing of Saturday came again.

My favorite part of preparing to go back to school was back-to-school shopping. That shopping trip was one of the grandest days of each summer. Number 2 pencils and a Snoopy pencil box plunged into the shopping buggy first that year, followed quickly by a box of 64 Crayolas with a built-in sharpener in the back. (I actually hated to color, but I adored picking up those crayons and taking in the differences of color – and I couldn't get enough of their smell! That rich box-just-opened scent that crept up your nose and somehow defined each and every color simultaneously by mere scent was simply divine!) Then two or three packs of notebook paper, always wide-ruled, although I longed for college-ruled paper. This was also the year I got a new three-ring binder. Most years there wasn't money for a new binder, no matter how ratty, beaten-up, or out-of-date it became from one school year to the next. This year, I chose one with a fluffy white kitten against a background of yellow roses. I loved cats, and I thought that this choice was solid and sensible, while practical and pleasing. I was set for school to begin.

"I sure hope you don't get ol' Miz Yates," Mom said at dinner one evening the week before school started back.

Mrs. Betty Jo Yates had been teaching school forever. Like my first grade teacher, Mrs. Fox, Mrs. Yates had taught at North Tazewell Elementary School since my mother had attended, at least twenty years ago. The same school secretary, Mrs. Kitts, was still there, too. Unlike Mrs. Fox and Mrs. Kitts, though, Mom didn't have anything good to say about Mrs. Yates.

Mom took another bite of her sandwich and shook her head, as if trying to awaken herself from some distant nightmare. "I remember how Mrs. Yates used to paddle those big ol' boys in sixth grade, biiiiiig ol' boys," she repeated for effect, "boys that shoulda already been in high school, but kept flunking. She'd paddle them so hard with her one good hand that she picked 'em plumb off the ground when her paddle connected with their bottoms! And you could hear them sobbing and crying out loud from one end of the school to the other!"

My eyes grew wide with fright just thinking of it. I almost whispered, "Why does she only have one hand, Mommy?"

"I don't really know," Mom said. "But she sure can be mean!"

I could not fathom how anyone – even big ol' boys like that – could deserve to be paddled so hard that they sobbed like babies! This was *not* a teacher that I wanted to get and I commenced to praying day and night that I would not.

The night before school started, we were at church
at the Light of Life Tabernacle (just like we were every
Sunday night – and Sunday morning and Wednesday
night), and Preacher Roy Lee called for people who wanted
to be anointed and prayed for to come to the front. I made
my way down the aisle, weaving in and out of women slain
in the spirit and men jumping and dancing about, speaking
in tongues, and I walked straight up front to the altar in
front of Preacher Roy Lee and Preacher Dean. I'd been
saved for years, since about second grade. I knew Bible
verses galore, mostly because the piano player was also our
Sunday school teacher and would buy the girls in class an
Aigner wallet (pronounced Ag-ner in our part of the world),
once we recited 100 verses. Doing so had only taken me
about a month. And I had sung with the choir, which
consisted almost exclusively of adults, since I was about
four years old.

Preacher Roy Lee bent low to me, as did Preacher
Dean, and asked what blessings I came seeking from God,
what answers to prayers I needed for God to send,
hallelujah. "I don't want Mrs. Yates for fifth grade," I
almost trembled as I said the words aloud. "I know that
God can deliver me from evil and I'm placing the matter in
His hands," I pronounced with great faith.

The two men stood and talked with each other
quickly and quietly before taking the bottle of anointing oil,
plugging it over with a thumb, turning it upside down, then
upright lightning-fast, and laid their hot hands on my
shoulders and began to pray for me. I never heard them
specifically tell God to deliver me from the fate of Mrs.
Yates as a teacher, but they did beseech Him to cover me in

His protective grace and mercy – I figured that had to be
the same thing – and the Holy Ghost seemed to be jumping
all over the two of them as they prayed, so I knew that I
must be safe now. *His will be done, amen!*

As Mom and I lay in bed in the dark that night and I
had said my prayers, thanking God for not giving me Mrs.
Yates for a teacher (I knew all about stepping out on faith),
she asked me what I would do if I did get Mrs. Yates. "Oh,
I've already talked to God and I had the preachers pray for
me tonight at church. I'll be just fine." But her asking me
this question planted a substantial seed of doubt in my mind
and I slept fitfully that night, my dreams filled with
potential scenarios that included Mrs. Yates paddling me in
such a way that she lifted my entire body from the ground,
and when she did so, I flew heavenward to be with Jesus.

North Tazewell Elementary had three teachers for
each grade. To find out which teacher you had been
assigned to, you went to the teacher's door and looked for
your name on an alphabetical list on the first day of school.
With the last name "Anderson," mine was typically the first
name on such a list.

"Mrs. Ratcliff, God, I'm begging you, Mrs.
Ratcliff," I chanted over and over and over on the bus, all
the way into the school, up to the crowd standing outside
the door of her classroom. Mrs. Ratcliff was the youngest
of the fifth grade teachers, pretty and fun. I waited my turn
and closed my eyes for a second of last-minute intercession
with Jesus before opening them to see my name – NOT on
the list of students for her class!

I felt as though someone had just pounded me in the
stomach, completely deflating my faith. Mr. Honeyak's

room was next door. A much smaller group was gathered there, as most kids had begun filing into their homerooms now. "God, I've never really given much consideration to Mr. Honeyak," I prayed silently, "but if this is your plan, then I will accept it and be glad." I walked straight up to the list outside his door. Again, my name was absent.

This could not be happening. I had prayed. I had diligently asked God to intervene on my behalf. I had been prayed over. I had believed! How could something like this happen in the face of all of that faith? I started to walk away down the hall. Maybe my name had accidentally been left off of the correct list. Yes, that had to be the answer. I headed toward the steps to go to the office to ask Mrs. Kitts to check for me. I passed Mrs. Yates' classroom on my way to the office, but I stayed as close to the library straight across the hall from her door as possible. I was almost to the stairs when I realized that someone was saying my name.

"Excuse me, aren't you Chrissy Anderson?"

I looked up and realized that it was Mrs. Yates. She was talking to me, addressing me by name. *She knew who I was!* She said it again, and stepped in front of me, stopping me in my tracks. "Um, yes, ma'am, I'm Chrissy Anderson."

"Well, where are you going, Chrissy?"

"I think that my name must have gotten left off of the classroom sheets. I didn't see it anywhere. So I'm going to ask Mrs. Kitts to help me find my teacher's room."

She smiled. It was not an evil smile, but one of confidence and perhaps even amusement and understanding. "Let's check to see if you're not on my list."

And with her good hand, she touched my shoulder and drew me over to the list beside her room. There it was, at the very top of the list. "Anderson, Christina." I couldn't decide whether to crumble into the floor or just cry. I looked up into her face, discouraged and defeated, and said, "I must have missed it there somehow."

She spoke clearly, but not with agitation or accusation, simply straightforwardness. "Or maybe you were hoping to be on another list and you didn't stop to check mine?"

She knew! Was she a mind reader of some sort? I remembered from a sermon that Preacher Roy Lee had delivered that those with that "gift" were evil, too. I didn't know what to think. I tried not to think so she wouldn't know what I was thinking. Words utterly failed me.

"It's okay, Chrissy, come on in," and she led me into the room, closing the door behind us, and taking me to my seat in the back of the first row, right beside her desk.

She walked from her desk to the front of the classroom, a brand new piece of chalk in hand. "Good morning, class!" She smiled, almost pleasantly, surveying the room, somehow making eye contact with each and every one of us before turning to write her name on the blackboard. "My name is Betty Yates. You will call me Mrs. Yates. And I'm very excited to have all of you in my class this year." She went on to tell us some of the things we could expect, things that the fifth grade classes always did before starting middle school next year. She also told us that every Friday afternoon, if we were good, we would join up with the other two fifth grade classrooms to have writing sessions over in the cafeteria. Sometimes we could write about whatever we wanted to, but other times, she or one of the other teachers would give us a topic. I remember sitting there spellbound by such a concept. I loved writing more than anything – and she liked it, too!?!? Could someone evil really appreciate writing like this? (Well, I reasoned, wasn't Satan over music in Heaven before God kicked him out? This was in another sermon by Preacher Roy Lee, where he explained why rock music was evil – because Satan was still in control of all music that wasn't church music or on the local country station.)

"I've noticed several of you – well, in truth, just about every one of you – looking at my hand. And my non-hand," Mrs. Yates announced, as she held her non-hand arm up for all to see. "Does anyone know what happened to my hand?"

All of us looked at each other. I'll bet every one of us had a guess, but no one was eager to share anything with her about what we might have heard.

She laughed quietly, "Oh, come on now, students. I'm sure that some of you have heard stories about why I only have one hand. Don't any of you have older brothers or sisters who might have told you?"

A skinny boy with blonde hair and a voice that came more from his nose than his throat, raised his hand. Mrs. Yates nodded at him to speak. "Well, my brother Joe said that it flew right off one day when you was paddling a boy for being bad!"

Mrs. Yates doubled over and laughed out loud. "Oh, I remember your brother and I can just imagine Joe telling you that! Well, it's a great story, but that's not the truth of it. And by the way, correct grammar would be 'when you *were* paddling a boy,' not 'when you was.' We'll work on that." She wiped a tear from her eye where she had been laughing so hard and asked if anyone else had heard a story about why she only had one hand.

Josh Fields asked if her family had been hungry and they had to cut it off to have food to eat. Mrs. Yates sorta made a face of disgust, and shook her head. "No, but that would be quite a horror story to write! Let's pray that none of us ever gets to that point. And boys and girls, if you're ever hungry and don't have food to eat, just come talk to me – don't cut off someone's hand." She winked, but there was something very sincere in her voice.

Otela Fox asked if her hand got torn off somehow while she was helping on her family's farm. She said that her uncle had lost part of a leg in a threshing accident once. "My, that's awful to hear," she answered, "and thankfully, no, my missing hand didn't happen through any sort of accident, although I'm sorry to hear about your uncle."

She waited a few minutes to entertain other ideas, but no one else spoke up. She smiled again and praised the ones who had spoken up. "I can see that I have some very creative students in class this year! Thank you for sharing these ideas with me today. Thank you for sharing stories about your own circumstances and your families. But see, the truth of the matter is really rather boring. I was just born without a second hand. Plain and simple. God just gave me one hand. What I want each of you to realize is that I do not consider myself a cripple and I do not wish for you to consider me one, either. I might only have one hand, but I can still do just about anything that anyone with two hands can do because I have taught myself to adapt – I've taught myself to manage just fine.

"I'm not exactly like the rest of you, but that is not necessarily a bad thing – just a different thing," she explained as she again held up the arm on which she had no hand and rubbed the rounded end of her wrist. "I will not tolerate students in my class making fun of people for their differences: *we're all different* from each other in some way. Some of you might be skinny and some of you might be fat. Some of you might be an only child and others may have several brothers and sisters. Some of you might come from a family that has a lot of money and others may not have much at all in terms of worldly possessions. All any of that means is that each of us has different life situations. Each of us deserves respect and kindness. Each of us deserves encouragement and uplifting. And in my classroom, these are the things that we will practice! Sure, we will learn social studies, grammar, spelling, and science, but my goal is for us to learn much more than what is contained within our textbooks. I want you to learn about life, about living, and how to share and grow from life experiences."

She paused a few moments to look around the room, to make sure that we followed what she was saying. "Some of you might have been afraid to come into my classroom this morning." She looked straight at me for a split second and I slunk down in my desk a little. "That isn't anything to be ashamed of. We're all afraid sometimes. But the best way to conquer fear of any kind is to meet it head-on! Sometimes the very things we were once most afraid of turn out to be the greatest learning experiences of our lives!"

I wrote Mrs. Yates a note at the end of that first day of fifth grade. *Thank you for being so nice and thank you for liking creativity. I want to be a writer when I grow up and I can't wait for Fridays in the lunchroom!*

The Funeral

I had never been in a mausoleum before. The dankness of the room numbed me, despite the sweltering early August heat outside. I stood beside my mother, statue-still. I did not want to be here – for so many reasons.

Funerals are not my forte. When I was a child, Mamaw and Papaw took me to funerals with them all the time. When you go to as many churches as we did when I was growing up, there seems to be someone dying every other week. Even as a small child, I recall the nausea that never failed to sweep over me at a funeral. From the moment I stepped into the funeral parlor, usually at Peery & St. Clair, my own breathing threatened to stop. The floral arrangements reached out to cut off the air, forbidding it to enter or leave my lungs. I would cough and hack and need to leave almost as soon as we arrived. Papaw said that the fresh flowers made my asthma act up; I strongly suspected that the flowers were really just trying to put me in a coffin, too.

So here I was, twenty-three years old, turning twenty-four in about two weeks. I had moved away from home to take a position as a Church Programmer in Roanoke, Virginia. It was my first "permanent" move, because the four years I had been at college didn't really count in my book. Not even a week after moving, my mother had called me one night. "Becky Hayes died last night."

I heard the words with perfect clarity. They breezed by me like a familiar song on the radio: you hear it, but it doesn't always sink in at first. Finally I found my voice. "Oh, gosh! What happened?"

"Her and that old Wilson boy that she was dating were on their way back from a concert of some kind – up around Roanoke, I think. It happened out at Gratton."

I took a long, deep breath. Becky Hayes had been my best friend in my youngest years. Our mothers, both "single moms" in a day and age before that was well-accepted, much less expected, worked together at Pyott-Boone. Becky's mom had never married Becky's father: Mom married my father, for all the good it did when he left before I turned six months old. Becky and I both lived with our mothers and our grandparents. Her granddaddy was a police officer in town. Her grandparents – and her mom, too, for that matter – cussed. We didn't talk like that at our house, so I always listened to Becky's family with fascination.

I remembered summer days before we ever started school. Our moms would put little swimsuits on us and send us out in the Hayes' front yard to play in Becky's blue plastic swimming pool with the plastic fish painted on the inside. That never lasted long, though. Becky and I would soon discard the swimsuits, running through the yard butt-naked and giggling our heads off as our mothers tried to catch us and wrap towels around us. Then we would put our regular clothes on and go outside with Popsicles to wait for darkness to fall so we could try to catch lightening bugs. While we waited, Becky would always look around to make sure her granddaddy wasn't watching and then we would sneak down to the little makeshift garage where her granny's big old car sat parked. (Becky's granny didn't venture out often, but when she did, she tended to scare those inside the car with her, as well as everyone she passed on the way.)

I was never good at sneaking, so she had to be extra-careful and act as look-out for me, too. And then she would take my hand and we would run over to the honeysuckle brambles beside that make-shift garage and she would inhale so deeply – I wondered how her insides didn't just explode she breathed in the fragrance so hard. Then she would tear off a blossom, tilt back her head, and suck the nectar through the bottom, smiling as if it were the sweetest taste on earth. I never wanted to do that. They were flowers. I could handle the smell okay, but preferred it from a distance. I certainly wasn't about to put it in my mouth like that! I knew for sure that they would kill me, no matter what she claimed. But that image of her with her head tilted back, sucking the blossom of the honeysuckle, smiling while wrapped in golden twilight stayed etched in my mind forever.

All of us teenagers drove too fast through Gratton, an out-of-the-way community in Tazewell. It was typically taken as a shortcut. A way to cut off some time and miles between Tazewell and anywhere else that could be reached via interstate highway. It was never a really safe road. Lots of hairpin turns, careening curves – all the dangerous stuff that kids love when they're that age. Add the adventure of excessive speed and it was like a natural high.

I didn't ask mom if there was drinking or drugs involved. I didn't need to. The fact that Becky had been with "that old Wilson boy" told me the answer. He hadn't even been hurt except a few scratches on his scrawny, white-trash face. All of the Wilsons were trouble. They always had been. The Wilsons were a lot like the Herdmans in that story about the Christmas pageant: they all looked alike – the boys and the one little girl, too – but were just different sizes with different black and blue marks on them from all the trouble they got into (with each other and anyone else they chose to pick a fight with). Alcohol and drugs were how a girl like the Becky I knew as a child ended up with someone like a Wilson in the first place.

By the time we were in middle school, Becky and I had different friends and were on different paths in life. By the time our high school years rolled around, we practically lived in different worlds. I do remember talking to her one time in high school. Only once in four whole years. I was in the upstairs girls' bathroom, puffing on an inhaler, when I realized that someone outside my stall was crying. Crying hard. I mean sobbing out loud like everything-in-life-that-was-good-was-gone crying. And I opened the door to see Becky there. She hadn't realized that anyone else was in the bathroom. Very quickly, she wiped her tears away, leaving a big ugly mascara streak all the way across her right cheek.

"Becky, are you okay?" I almost whispered.

"Of course I'm okay," she retorted. "Why wouldn't I be okay? Why do you wanna know?"

I shrugged my shoulders and stammered, "I – I – I just wondered if you were okay. I heard you crying."

"Bullshit!" she practically spat at me. "I wasn't crying!" She paused before asking, "Do you have any smokes? I need one."

Of course I didn't have any smokes. She knew that.
Then she looked at me, glaring at me with a look of disdain
that I would never forget. "You don't have anything I need
– there's nothing that you could do to help me, even if you
really wanted to!" And she huffed out of the bathroom,
leaving me standing there feeling like I had been the one
who was crying.

I didn't want to go to the funeral. Mom guilt-tripped
me into it. She didn't want to go by herself. She was so
thankful to still have me. I don't think she even stopped to
consider how it might make Becky's mom feel to see me
there with Mom. I mean, Becky and I were the same age.
And I was standing there, alive and well, while Becky was
closed up in a coffin, gone from her side forever. But I
went.

I sat through the service, still numb. Thoughts spun
a hundred miles an hour in my mind, completely out of
control, just like their car had been the night she died. I
watched her mom sit there and try not to cry for the loss of
her only child, too soon after losing both of her own
parents. I watched two police officers bring in Becky's
estranged husband, a former police officer who had been
convicted on forgery charges, the chains around his ankles
clanging, the sound echoing off the mausoleum walls. I
watched his and Becky's son look from his father to the
coffin, then up at Becky's mom. I watched Becky's
youngest child, supposedly the son of that old Wilson boy,
wiggle on his grandmother's lap. And I kept wondering,
"How can I be here? How can these things have
happened?"

And I cried. I finally sobbed aloud, just
like Becky had that one time I'd spoken to her in high
school. I felt the loss in a way that nearly sickened me
worse than all of those fresh-cut flowers. But I did not
weep for that woman in the coffin. I couldn't cry for her – I
didn't even know her. I wept for that little girl at twilight,
leaning her head back and sucking out every drop of
goodness the honeysuckle had to offer. I wept for a
childhood friendship that had already been lost to me for
most of my twenty-three years.

Something Stupid

"Do you know why you're here, Amanda?" The doctor's voice was slow and deliberate.

Amanda Martin weighed her options and answered in a low, defeated, utterly flat tone, "Because I did something stupid."

Since her husband James had driven her the short distance from their split-level to the Medical Center, Amanda had answered this question so many times it truly wasn't even funny. Not even to that scathing sense of sarcasm that typically got her through every life situation she needed it to. She had marveled from the beginning how *naturally* the answer came. "Because I did something stupid." Yes, it was true, but that didn't make up for the fact that the answer was absolutely ludicrous! Yet, instinctively, she knew it was what everyone wanted to hear.

Dr. Latté – honest to God, that's what his name tag read – looked pensive. He seemed to accept her answer before prodding gently. "And what was that, Amanda? What did you do that was stupid, precisely?"

She breathed deeply, choking back the acridity of it, trying to sound remorseful rather than disappointed, praying she would be able to pull this off with yet another medical professional. "I tried to kill myself."

Dr. Latté stared down at the chart in front of him, shaking his head (as if his disappointment meant anything to her). "Why would you do that?"

This question infuriated her. "Because I'm tired!" *Anger won't get you out of here*, she quickly reminded herself, then tried again. "Because I'm so very tired," she almost whispered.

"What are you tired of?"

*It'd be a hell of a lot faster to tell you what I'm **not** tired of,* she snapped internally. Running her fingers through her short hair, she recollected the recent night when another "meltdown" hit her and she took a pair of kitchen shears to her hair. She remembered watching her face contort in the mirror as she realized what she had done, seeing the tears before she felt them on her cheeks, blinding her already imperfect vision. She had crumpled like a butterfly against a speeding car's windshield. Concocting a story to tell her hairdresser was challenging, but she pulled it off beautifully, weaving a convincing tale about a cousin's mischievous child cutting it while she napped after a family dinner.

Amanda realized that Dr. Latté was waiting for her response. "What am I tired of?" she repeated, trying to laugh. "Well, I think mostly, I'm just tired. I'm tired of fighting with James. Of not having anyone to communicate with. Of him being irresponsible with money. I'm tired of not being able to believe him because he lies all the time and he's a terrible liar." *Unlike myself,* she wanted to add, but resisted. She laughed to herself when she thought of all the times she had point-blank told others, "You can't lie to a liar: we'll see through it every time, even when we don't really want to." She looked up at the doctor. "But really, I'm mostly just tired. I just want to go home and sleep."

And that was true. That was what started this whole mess. She and James had gotten into another argument about money. The fact that he didn't want her to worry or be upset was sweet – except that he never managed to keep everything covere. Then she found out about whatever they were short on *and* that he had lied.

She remembered driving, angry and crying, stupefied by the fact that she had worked so hard to get a good education, to escape her suffocating little hometown, to find just the right man to marry, not settling for some local boy when she was fresh out of high school or even college. Yet, here she was, 33, nearly five years into a marriage with someone who lied to her about money – making her lifelong dream of security impossible to achieve. It wasn't that she didn't love James. On the contrary, she loved him with almost every fiber of her being. If not for the communication and financial problems, he would have been damn near perfect.

Loving him was probably what saved her life last night. She returned home from her drive bitterly angry. The van that James had insisted they buy with their IRS refund the year before – the van he assured her was in good shape and that died in K-Mart's parking lot the evening of purchase – still sat in the driveway, a visible reminder of James' miserable inability to make rational decisions involving money. Add to that the fact that the IRS had also informed the Martins that there was an error on that same refund and they owed Uncle Sam about $1500, and it was easy to understand her hatred towards it. She nicknamed it "The Money Pit" because that was what it was. And it didn't matter where James parked it – in the backyard, it laughed at her daily from her bathroom window; in the driveway, it mocked her and bore witness to the whole neighborhood that life in the split-level was far from perfect. She screamed obscenities at the van as she keyed the letters (M-O-N-E-Y-P-I-T) down the side facing the neighbors' house.

Then she stomped up the drive and dramatically jumped to grab the UT windsock that James had carelessly burned cigarette holes into for the past 18 months, not on purpose, but simply because he was quite tall and didn't pay attention. She had asked him repeatedly to take it down. At 6'4", it certainly would've been an easier feat for him than for her stubby little 5'5" frame. She grabbed a cigarette lighter from the front seat of his car and set the windsock on fire, laughing hysterically as it burned and disappeared before her maniacal glare. That's when she realized that she had not only pulled down the windsock, but also the flag pole. "Here's to being free!" she screamed through clenched teeth and tore the American flag from the broken pole as she smashed the wood against the pavement, splintering it further before launching it like a javelin into the cold December nighttime.

After the tirade, she felt almost calm. She walked up the front stairs, slamming the door. James was in the den downstairs and didn't answer, probably hoping she had driven around long enough to accept the latest financial woes and lies. Amanda hadn't lingered long on the landing, walking silently down the hall to her office.

A recent Christmas gift sat on her desk. She picked it up, crying. A journal. She was sure her cousin meant well. After all, Amanda had always loved writing. It should have been a perfect gift! But instead, it reminded her of how much more stable her life was before marrying James, before taking on his lackadaisical approach to finances as

part and parcel of her own life. She had always told her
mother that she would rather be happy and alone than
married and miserable. Yet here she sat.

As she rummaged through her drawer in search of a
pen to start writing down these very thoughts, she found the
medicine bottle. A bottle of hot-pink horse pills, prescribed
for back spasms months earlier. Amanda suddenly realized
that she just wanted to sleep. She was tired of the fighting,
the lies, the money issues and overall insecurity. And these
pills had always been great at helping her relax, perfect for
helping her rest. So why not take a couple? She counted
two and popped them into her mouth, not even leaving the
room for a glass of water. *Choke it down, Amanda,* she
coaxed. Then she thought, *If two make me relax, what
would three do? How about four?* She kept swallowing
pills, even after she quit counting at twelve. She hadn't
started out to end things at all, and certainly not like this,
but now that it was done, there was one last burst of fury.
With finality, she marched to the top of the stairs and
screamed, "I hate you, James Martin! I hate you!"

She half-stumbled back down the hall, pulling her
worn-out body onto their bed, knowing it would all be over
soon. As she lay there, beginning to fade away, she
suddenly felt guilty. Not guilty for taking the pills or for
wanting to never wake up. But guilty for those last words to
James. Because they simply were not true. And she knew it
could not end like this. She could not leave this world with
him thinking she hated him when it wasn't the truth.
Amanda drowsily walked downstairs to the edge of the den,
without going in. She forced herself not to look at him. She
didn't want to do anything that might change her unplanned

decision. She spoke quietly, purposefully. "James, I'm sorry I said that. I don't hate you. I've never hated you, and I never will. I'm so sorry. But it'll all be okay. I promise. It will all be okay by tomorrow." There were no new tears. Just those few words and she went back to bed, pulling the covers up tight around her.

But James was more perceptive than she imagined. Sitting on the edge of the bed, he tried to rouse her. "Amanda, what do you mean? What do you mean that everything will be all right by tomorrow? What have you done?" His shaking wasn't angry, more like urgent. She finally muttered about the pills. Once he had ascertained that "a few" was way more than she should have taken, he forced her out of bed, practically dragging her to the car, and driving the three minutes it took to get to the Med Center.

"What happened?" the ER attendant asked.

"She took Darvocet. At least a dozen," James answered calmly.

The attendant looked up into Amanda's glassy eyes, "Mrs. Martin, what did you do?"

The words had floated effortlessly as Amanda hung her head, ashamed of the answer, but not denying it. "I did something stupid."

Most of the night was a blur. She remembered the nurse trying to keep her talking, forcing charcoal-liquid-nastiness down her to neutralize the pills. How ironic that all she wanted was sleep, the one thing that everyone seemed determined to deny her! How ironic that the very man whose irresponsibility had driven her to this sat beside her every moment, talking quietly, explaining everything from his medical viewpoint as an EMT, holding her hand, comforting her, promising that it really would be all right by tomorrow.

Blue Ridge Acres was the closest psychiatric facility and the ER staff demanded that she be admitted there since their psych wing was full that night. At the Acres, there was more paperwork, then the news that James couldn't accompany her past the elevator. She was amazed at the few possessions permitted – nearly everything was considered dangerous, including her contacts' saline solution.

She settled into her room around 5:30, after being told that group therapy would begin at 7:00. The fact that she landed here out of a desire for sleep and *rest* loomed large and practically guffawed in her face. "Look," she calmly reasoned, "I'm really, really tired. I've been awake for almost twenty-four hours. You can wake me up at 7:00 if you want, but I won't take part in anything even remotely resembling group therapy until I can rest awhile. Sleep deprivation doesn't incline me to share and play nice." It hadn't really been an ultimatum – simply the truth. Begrudgingly, they agreed to let her sleep until 9:00, just in time for the second group session.

But at 6:30, someone knocked quietly and entered Amanda's room. "Ms. Martin, I'm sorry to bother you, but there seems to be a problem with your insurance. Blue Ridge Acres isn't accepted on your plan. We need to move you to another facility. Would you prefer –?"

Amanda raised her head from the pillow in the too-sterile room in utter disbelief. "What you are telling me," she uttered in calm, even syllables, "is that the ER sent me *here* after I tried to kill myself over financial issues, and this – *facility*," she nearly spat the word, "isn't covered on my insurance and now I'm going to have to pay for being here *out of my own pocket*? Un-be-lieve-able." Each syllable came out as if a separate word. Amanda plopped back onto the pillow. She shook her head in disbelief for several moments before noticing the woman was still there. Amanda forced a deep breath out slowly, answering quietly, "You know what? Get them to release me, send me home, and I'll just go to bed there." Sleep seemed destined to be denied, so she might as well focus on doing whatever was necessary to get out of here. She noticed the door had no lock. For obvious reasons, of course, but its absence somehow made her feel quite vulnerable.

Around 8:45, she was notified that the doctor was reviewing her file and would see her "shortly," but she should go to the group session until he sent for her.

Amanda chose a seat away from everyone else. Another irony. Typically, she was the social director among her friends and peers, always in the middle of the action. James playfully told her once that it was "better to be a social butterfly than a social disease." Now she decided she'd rather be seen as the latter during what she prayed would be a short stay at the Acres.

The group leader invited her to sit closer to the group. Amanda's voice quivered slightly as she politely declined the invitation, explaining that she was waiting for the doctor to call her out. The leader smiled patronizingly, shrugged, and turned to the group. "Okay, then, we'll go ahead and get started." She turned to a smallish man sitting the farthest away. "Matt," she said warmly, "let's start with you this morning. Why are you here?"

"Because I did something stupid," the man's voice eked out of his tiny frame.

Amanda sat in stunned silence. *It must be that automatic for everyone, then. How are we programmed to know that's what they want to hear? Apology and remorse, even if we don't mean it!* She listened as Matt explained how he had slit his wrists to avoid dealing with life.

The next person up was a big guy named Michael. "Michael, why are you here?"

"Oh, 'cos I did something stupid. I still don't really understand it. I mean, it *was* stupid – and absolutely unacceptable! I've been hunting and shooting since I could hold a gun. How the hell I missed my sorry-ass brother-in-law from ten yards away is *still* beyond me!" He laughed a great big belly-laugh, shaking his head, still in disbelief. Amanda simultaneously respected him for not bowing to the whims of what he was obviously *expected* to say, but also realized with renewed urgency that she couldn't spend a night here. Michael was funny, but also potentially dangerous.

Just then, Amanda was escorted to Dr. Latté's office, where she still waited to see if he would grant her a reprieve, clemency for a first-time offender in the realm of suicide attempts. "You know, Amanda," he looked up from her chart and into her eyes, "it's really difficult for me to release you, knowing that you're probably not going to check into another facility where you can be helped. I know you want out of here – badly. You feel like you don't belong here – and maybe you don't – but the fact remains that you did something very reckless. You tried to kill yourself. That is – to say the least – pretty serious stuff. And to release you into the care of the person you've told me seemed to be the driving force of your decision to end your life..." He met her gaze. "I'm not sure that's best. Maybe not for you *or* James."

Panic threatened. Amanda desperately did not need this in addition to her fears of being locked up with crazy people. She took a deep breath, praying he would see that home was the best place for her. "Look, Dr. Latté..." She paused, pleased that she had managed to say his name without even the slightest hint of a snicker. "I really want to go home. I'm so incredibly tired and I just – need to sleep. I promise I'm not going to do anything stupid again. And as for James, well, if it hadn't been for James, I might not even have gotten this second chance. He's the one who realized what was going on and got me to the ER. He'll be watching – he won't let anything happen." She still wasn't sure if that was a comfort or a liability, but either way, it was true. James would watch her. Nothing would happen that shouldn't happen. She was quite certain that all "dangerous" medications (likely anything stronger than Tylenol or Aleve) had been disposed of or hidden from her reach at home. "Please," her voice almost ached as she pleaded once more, "just let me go home to get some rest."

After a few minutes of scanning her chart, Dr. Latté put down the folder. "Amanda, I'm going to go ahead and let you go home. But you and James really need to get into some counseling. It sounds like it might be something that would help both of you, as well as the marriage."

How could she explain that she hated shrinks and that James wouldn't talk to anyone about anything private or personal? She couldn't. She shouldn't. Most importantly, she wouldn't. She closed her eyes, agreeing with his assessment, which she believed was probably accurate. She knew it wouldn't happen, but yes, it probably would help. She tried not to look too eager as she asked, "Can I call home, then? Can James come get me now?"

And as the doctor nodded his head, Amanda thought to herself, *I guess all of us do stupid things.*

Retail Hell

"Retail hell, retail hell, someone shoot me now!" Rita Jo sang to the tune of "Jingle Bells" as she kicked off her high heels under the desk in her office in the Ever-Busy Bookstore on the Friday before Christmas. With exactly one week left until Christmas Day, she wondered if she was going to make it!

Rita Jo Patton stood five-foot-one if when perfectly erect, thus the abominable high heels that now lay sideways at her feet. With natural chestnut curls that hung more than halfway down her back, impeccable make-up at all times, and great big brown eyes that could melt an iceberg, Rita Jo was a woman of exquisite beauty. But there was more to Rita Jo than mere good looks. She had a fashion sense that could put Paris Hilton to shame. She wore her intelligence wrapped closely about her, like a red silk scarf that people notice and admire, without it taking center stage. And her voice…. Rita Jo had a voice that was like warm honey comingled with smooth whiskey on a cold winter's day – and that voice could woo or wound completely, depending on how she chose to deal with the situation at hand. Moreover, all of these combined with her prowess in sales to make her a force to be reckoned with at the Ever-Busy Bookstore on any day, but especially so during the busy-ness of the holidays.

"Hey, Rita Jo!" manager Pete Coffey called out as he walked into her office unannounced, without the courtesy of even knocking beforehand. "Have you seen these sales stats?"

"For the love of God, Pete, could you at least knock before you come barging in? Geez, I might have been on a phone call or doing something private! Were you raised in a barn or something?" She slugged back the last of her cup of coffee and glared at him as menacingly as possible.

"Well, I knew you weren't on the phone – your line wasn't lit up when I left my office. As for doing something private, well, we're too busy to do anything private until after January 1st!" He paused as she rolled her eyes at him, and then continued. "So, anyway, back to these sales stats…. We're the on verge of breaking last year's holiday record! With the economy what it is right now, I have no clue how this is the case, but take a look."

She grabbed the report from his hands and leaned over to study it. "How in the world? Pete, are you sure these numbers are legit? Is someone on the floor yanking your chain again?"

Her reference to a practical joke from a couple of years ago that had Pete going for nearly a week made him blush and mumble something very un-festive under his breath before going on. "No, Rita Jo, I swear! These are straight from home office!"

Still not believing him, she pulled up an electronic version of what she held in her hands on her computer. "O Holy Night!" Rita Jo whooped and jumped up. "Pete, we're gonna get us a big ol' Christmas bonus if we stay on track! Wonder what it will be?" Already, she had visions of a big, black Mercedes dancing through her head.

"You really think we can pull it off? What if –"

"'What if' what? Don't you go jinxing this for us! This staff *needs* this Christmas bonus, Pete. They *deserve*

this bonus. And you and I are gonna work like wildfire
until closing time on Christmas Eve to make sure that they
get this Christmas bonus! Do you understand?"

"Well, um, I do, but –"

"No 'buts," Pete! Just yours and mine working
themselves down to nothing, you hear? Customers,
customers, customers! Sales, sales, sales! Do you believe in
Christmas miracles, Pete? Do you? Unless you're gonna
say yes, don't bother opening your mouth! Just follow my
lead, because Rita Jo's leading your sales sleigh *this year*,
Santa!" And with that, she was back in her heels and
pulling Pete out the door to greet customers and up-sell like
crazy.

For the next five days, Rita Jo and Pete made a
point to deck the halls with their helpfulness. If someone
looked confused about whether to buy book A or book B
and Rita Jo got within five feet, chances were excellent that
both books were going home with the customer! And if
someone liked that leather-bound diary, Pete had three
more must-buy items to accompany it, and all rang up like
heavenly choirs singing! The pair of them inspired all of
the sales associates. Santa's elves had never worked more
efficiently or pleasantly. Rita Jo got goose bumps just
thinking of how all of this hard work might pay off!

On the morning of December 24th, Rita Jo realized
that breaking last year's record hung in the balance; it could
go either way. Today had to be perfect. People had to come
in looking for something and leaving with more. She honed
her senses to detect credit cards needing to be freed from
tightly-clasped wallets and purses. She was on her game
200%.

And then she got into her 2002 Ford Focus and the damned thing wouldn't start! "Oh, no, you don't," she said through gritted teeth. "You *cannot* do this to me. Not today, Gladys, do you understand me? Today is far too important and *everything* must go right! Start, Gladys! I command you to start!" Again, the engine refused to turn over and chugged pathetically. "Gladys," Rita Jo tried to speak calmly this time, "if you do not start *this instant*, I am going to trade you in, do you hear me? I'm gonna trade you in for something long and sleek and lovely and German! Start, Gladys! Start right now!"

Out of the corner of her eye, Rita Jo saw her neighbor Steve smiling at her bemusedly. "Hey, Steve," she rolled down her window, "think you could jump my car off? I've gotta get to work. It's Christmas Eve and I've got a lot to do!"

"Sure thing. I'll be right back with the jumper cables."

"Thanks, babe, I owe you one!" She jumped out of the car to have a quick smoke while she waited. Maybe that would calm her down a little, sooth her nerves. Rita Jo shook out her luxurious hair as she lit the cigarette and almost immediately started jumping around, pounding herself in the side of the head. "Oh, hell fire!" She felt the warmth of the match get a little too close to her overly-moussed-and-sprayed coif, and the smell of burning hair alarmed her, to say the least. Then a spark fell from the cigarette and landed on her black leather coat and she threw it off as she flung her cigarette to the ground, trying to make sure no damage came to the coat or the rest of her.

Steve looked at her in bewilderment as he pulled his pick-up into her driveway. "Good Lord, Rita Jo! What're you doing? Taking off your clothes or something? It's too cold out here to be streakin'!" He laughed a great-big belly laugh and shook his head as he attached the cables to her battery.

"I'm not streaking, Steve, no such luck for you!" she teased. "This is as close to naked as you will ever see me, my dear man! My stupid cigarette dropped onto my coat and I singed my hair with the match when I was lighting up," Rita Jo explained as she got back into her car and waited for Steve's signal to crank her up.

"Well, Rita Jo, a gal as pretty as you don't need to be smoking no-how. And if this is as close to naked as I'll ever see you, then I reckon you're naked enough!"

She couldn't help but smile at him as the engine turned and he grinned at her. "What time you get off tonight, Rita Jo?" Steve called above the revving of her engine.

"We close at 6, why? You gonna come buy some books today?"

"Hell, no," Steve guffawed. "I just figure I better be close-by so you're not stuck at the store for Christmas. That battery's just about done for, girl!"

Traffic was already backed up getting onto the interstate, so she took the back way to work. It took a little longer, but she would still make it on time. She tried to steady her breathing and think relaxing thoughts. She listened to a local radio station that had been playing all Christmas music since before Thanksgiving. Back when she had been in radio they sure couldn't get by with that!

No matter, those days of sales in radio were behind her. And if today went well at Ever-Busy Books, she could be behind the wheel of that new Mercedes in no time flat!

She pulled into the parking lot to find an ambulance pulled up to the store. "Oh, good Lord, what is going on?" she cried out as she ran to the front entrance.

She saw that the medics had Pete stretched out in front of them. "Pete, what in the world are you doing?"

"I kinda fell, Rita Jo," Pete tried to explain. "I was helping our first customer carry out some bags of books and –"

"Where's the customer?" Rita Jo looked around. "Did you fall on the way to or from helping? Did the customer get all of the stuff okay?"

"Yes, the customer is fine, Rita Jo! *I'm* the one who's injured!"

One of the medics announced that Pete had broken his leg – in two different places. Rita Jo closed her eyes and asked, "Does this mean that he can't work today?"

The medic tried not to laugh. "Yes, ma'am, I'm afraid it does."

Rage built within her. Today, of all days! Now she was gonna have to rely on no one other than herself to see this through. She could feel the headache building behind her eyes as she heard a voice from her past saying, "This must be what it feels like when an aneurism starts!" She took a deep breath, and opened her eyes to look beyond Pete and the ambulance attendants. A crowd of about 30 people was trying to get a gander at Pete. These people wanted to see some action, so that's what they were gonna get!

Rita Jo put on her best holiday sales smile and let her voice work for her. "Hey, everyone, let's give Pete here some quality time with these medical professionals! Come on in the store and warm up a little. Tell the folks back in the café that I said to give you all a cup of coffee – it's just freezing out here."

The crowd moved inside and she ushered them in from behind. She grabbed a sales clerk and said, "Call the café – tell them to ring all of these coffees on my number and I'll pay them when I get inside. Thanks, hon!" She looked back at Pete. "If I ever find out that you did this on purpose –"

"Rita Jo," Pete winced as the medics raised the gurney into the back of the ambulance, "who would do something like this on purpose?"

Before the drivers could take off, Rita Jo invited them in for a quick cup of coffee. Much to her surprise – and Pete's dismay – they agreed and followed her inside. They left with calendars for all of their families and friends. Rita Jo was stressed, but smiling all the way to the check-out counter.

Just after the ambulance left the parking lot, Rita Jo broke a nail. Right down into the quick – no hope for fixing it. And within another hour, she had paper-cut herself three times. At lunch, she spilled spaghetti on her winter-white blouse and had to go to her office to change clothes. The registers were ringing sales, but by 2:00 in the afternoon, the crowds had dwindled to a few people scavenging through the bargain bins or looking for very specific items.

One lady informed her that she *knew* the store had a certain book in stock – she had seen it on their website.

Rita Jo tried to be polite as she explained, "Ma'am, I'm sorry, but our store doesn't actually own that website. We share a name, but not necessarily the same stock."

"Well, that's just stupid!" the lady yelled at her.

Rita Jo tried to laugh and keep her cool. "I know, I know. It's just crazy. Hey, tell you what, let's see what we have here in the store that's similar to that author. You know, I've been reading this author over here and I really love his work!" By the time the lady left, she had spent $200 on authors she'd never heard of and books she might never read. But as Rita Jo helped her scan the shelves, they suddenly seemed like the most fascinating reading material on earth!

Around 3:00, Rita Jo decided that the shelves needed straightening before the last-minute shoppers arrived, likely around 5:00. She loathed straightening the shelves. Things never stayed in order long and it always seemed like a waste of time. But it was a *necessary* waste of time, she knew. If bookshelves looked nice, people were more apt to approach and browse; if people approached and browsed, they were much more likely to purchase; if people purchased, sales went up; if sales went up, Rita Jo might get a new set of wheels!

A gentleman approached her at about this time. "Excuse me, do you work here?"

Do I work here? Rita Jo thought to herself. *I have a nametag around my neck that is the size of the board that you hold up when the nice little police officer is booking you (not that I know anything about having a mug shot taken, mind you). I have a set of keys on my arm that weighs more than I do. I have a phone on my hip with a*

*great big Ever-Busy Books logo on it. And I am putting
books on the shelf in front of me. Do I work here???*

"*Do I work here?*" she managed to laugh as she said
it. She took the gentleman's arm as though they were long-
lost friends. "Honey, I *do* work here and I can't wait to help
you find what you are looking for!" Thirty minutes later,
the gentleman left with a cold mocha frappe in one hand
and *Twilight* box sets for his eight granddaughters, a new
Bible for his wife, and gift certificates for all of his
neighbors.

Around 4:00, a guy came in and asked, "Hey, you
got a bathroom?"

"No, we sure don't! But there's a Johnny Blue at
the end of the parking lot. Do you have four quarters on
you?" The man stared at her, obviously lost. She met his
blank stare with a grin, as she suddenly realized that her
"inside voice" had gotten out! "Oh, sweetie, I'm just
kidding you! Walk right back here with me and I'll show
you where it is." *Besides that,* she thought to herself, *I
don't wanna go shocking you and have to clean up
anything*! On his way out, Rita Jo stopped him to apologize
for her bizarre sense of humor when he had asked about the
restroom. "It's just been a long day, hon, you know?"

"Oh, I know. We have a new baby and I just can't
seem to get the hang of this new-dad thing."

Rita Jo to the rescue! The guy left with books on
parenting, fatherhood, and so much more! As well as
scrapbooking materials for his young wife so they could
capture every moment of their time with that precious new
baby.

At 5:00, just as anticipated, the store was suddenly jammed with last-minute shoppers. Rita Jo moved from customer to customer offering suggestions and bookseller insights. She even helped at the registers when needed for a brief fifteen-minute interlude. The last hour of the workday was not much more than a blur. A beautiful cash-colored, credit-card inscribed blur!

When the announcement was made for "Fifteen minutes 'til closing," Rita Jo went quickly to her office to shut down the computer she had never managed to even sit behind on this last day before Christmas. She noticed a new email and thought, "Just a quick look." And there it was: an email from the home office announcing what the big Christmas bonus would be for the stores that matched last season's holiday sales. Her eyes hurriedly skimmed through the email, seeking out dollar signs, but none readily appeared. She started at the beginning, reading it carefully. The last sentence leaped off the screen and she sank into her office chair in utter disbelief. She just shut off the computer, not bothering to log off or anything. Just shut it off and walked towards the front of the store, still reeling from the shock. She had worked so hard, so diligently. And for what? A $250 Ever-Busy Bookstore gift card! That *may* pay off what she now owed to the café for all of those free coffees she gave the crowds this morning.

In those last moments before closing, a man ran through the doors looking frazzled and forsaken. "Do you have any books?"

Rita Jo waited. Books about what? Books by whom? Books for which occasions? Books pertaining to places or people? "I'm sorry," she finally responded when the man had no further descriptions about what kinds of books he might be looking for. "Everything you see here is make-believe. There are no books in this store."

She grunted "Merry Christmas" to her fellow Ever-Busy Bookstore associates and made her way to the back edge of the parking lot, to her beloved Ford Focus, Gladys, who she hoped had forgiven her by now for even *thinking* of trading her in for a silly black Mercedes.

Corey's Quarry: Killer Rocks and Gemstones

From the moment my boyfriend Nicky and I hit the city limits sign of Salem, Massachusetts, an unspoken excitement swirled through the air. The carnival-like atmosphere caught us up from the time the car doors opened. Frivolity abounded. We made our way towards a costume shop called "The Lion, The Witch, & Their Wardrobe." The elaborateness of some of the costumes surprised me. I saw everything from cheap plastic masks and capes to authentic-looking Victorian dresses and shoes. I couldn't imagine spending the money and time that some must have taken to look as utterly chic as they appeared in their shops, stands, and just standing on the street corners of the little centuries-old town. Cackling filled the air alongside the laughter of teenagers, and the occasional cries of a younger child caught off-guard by someone in a spooky costume wandering by.

Nicky led me into shop after shop bearing witty, witchy and supernatural names: things like a tea shop called The Witch's Brew, and general goods and wares outlets with names like Wicked Goodz, Spell-Binder, Charmed, B-Witched, and The Cat, The Crow, and the Crown. Also lining the streets were numerous shops advertising psychic readings, and haunted houses. At the end of one street, seemingly remote and quiet, I saw a rather plain-looking storefront lettered "Corey's Quarry: Killer Rocks and Gemstones." Just reading the name bothered me, dousing the fun-filled euphoria that had wrapped me up tightly since arriving in Salem.

"What's wrong?" Nicky asked. "You okay?"

I looked back up at the sign, pointing it out to him. "Wasn't Giles Corey one of the people accused of witchcraft?"

He nodded. "Yeah, he was an old guy, about 80. He refused to plead innocent *or* guilty so they couldn't try him. Instead of facing the gallows, being burned at the stake, being drowned or something horrible like happened to the others, he was pressed to death – they piled rocks on him until he died."

"And how long did that take?" I asked in disgust.

"Like two days," Nicky answered quietly. A moment later, he leaned over and nuzzled my ear, kissing me gently. "Ah, come on, Cille. It's just a play on words. Just an advertising gimmick. I'm sure it's nothing personal."

I looked at the sign again and shook my head, trying to smile and shrug it off. "I guess."

"Trust me," he smiled. "I'm the tour director here, right?"

We continued up and down the streets for another couple of hours, in and out of more storefronts and specialty shops. After a while, Nicky suggested that we grab a bite to eat somewhere. I agreed that we should have something more than cotton candy or chocolate bars by this time in the evening. Even the more substantial food fares insisted on the hokey names pertaining to the town's infamous past, but The Black Cat sounded harmless enough.

After dinner, Nicky and I strolled back along the streets, less crowded now that night had fallen, but now inhabited largely by teenagers laughing raucously and recklessly, pointing at various passersby, half-threatening anyone who looked in their direction a moment or two too long. Nicky's arm wrapped around me a little more tightly, promising security and safety from the brooding elements skulking about.

I could see Corey's Quarry coming up again and there was some sort of activity going on in the alley beside the store. Three strapping linebacker-looking teens that smelled of beer and boredom had cornered a smaller, geeky-looking teen-aged boy against the side of the building. The smaller guy looked terrified and I really couldn't blame him. The three hulking figures stood over him, spewing bravado. I quickened my pace and the three bullies ran into Corey's Quarry, leaving the geeky guy to flee in the opposite direction. Without waiting to make sure that Nicky was behind me, I ran in to report the scene we had just witnessed outside, fully expecting to point out the teens to the store manager.

Once inside the store, however, I saw no one at all. The teens were nowhere in sight; no store manager greeted me at the door. All around me were lovely crystals, geodes, fossils, and gems of all types lining jewelry cases. Various other gift items caught my eye as I looked around the store, which I now realized was filled with lovely purple light. I looked up and around in wonderment, completely lost in the magic and beauty all around me. Nicky was suddenly beside me, asking if I was okay.

"It's so beautiful," I whispered, still dazed by the unnatural beauty of each item I observed. I carefully picked up a music box and opened the lid to hear one of my favorite childhood lullabies.

Nicky came up and hugged me from behind. "Not exactly what I expected from the outside; how about you?"

"Not at all," I admitted, still a little breathless.

Just then, a woman appeared, as if from thin air. She approached us, smiling. Her name tag read "Chelsea."

"Hello," she greeted. "Welcome to Corey's Quarry. Is there anything I can help you with this evening?"

"I, uh, I – " I really couldn't decide what to say. I could have mentioned that I thought the name of the store was simply hideous and wrong; I could have mentioned that I only came in because I was chasing three big guys who had a defenseless little guy trapped in the alley outside; I could have even told her how magnificent the store was, if I'd been able to find the words to do so. Instead, I simply stammered and stood there.

She laughed softly and waved us over to a floor display of seemingly plain field stones. "A lot of people – ones in the know, like yourselves, anyway –" she clarified, "are put off by the name of the store. I'm glad you decided to come in, even if it was just to chase off those misbehaving boys."

I looked at her, stunned. I looked at Nicky, who seemed just as surprised as I was. "How did you know –" I started, but stopped. "Where did the boys go?"

"Oh, they won't be bothering anyone for quite some time, I assure you. This isn't the first time and I made good on my promise to make sure it doesn't happen again." For a moment, her smile had almost vanished, but now it returned, fresh and soothing. And as for what you were thinking?" she laughed quietly, seemingly embarrassed. "There I go again," she shook her head. "I don't do it intentionally, but I sometimes kinda know what people are thinking and respond to that instead of waiting to see what they actually say. I'm very sorry."

She looked back at the display of rocks and stones before them, "Giles Corey was one of my ancestors. He was married three times, so there are loads of us who can trace our lineages back to him," she smiled. "Well, anyway, Giles owned some land and transferred ownership of it to two sons-in-law before his rather untimely demise. That didn't leave much for most of his other children, grandchildren, and the rest of us." She smiled and turned back to the display. "I'm the sort of person who believes we're dealt a certain hand in life for a reason. And we can either complain about it or do something with it. Giles' last words are where I draw my strength in life," she went on. "'More weight.' Can you even imagine that? You're being murdered oh so slowly and painfully, and rather than cave to what your persecutors want you to say, rather than admitting to some trumped-up charge that they have created against you, rather than verbalizing something that might at least temporarily end your pain, you say over and over again, 'More weight.' Isn't that amazing strength?"

I had never considered it that way. Giles Corey had always seemed a helpless victim to me. But in this light, he became a hero for standing his ground, even though he was trapped prostrate with boulders, rocks, and stones of all sizes heaped upon his chest to push the life out of him.

"To add further insult," she went on, "they buried him in an unmarked grave, forbidding that it be marked in any way. But people knew. Someone always knows," she added with a twinkle in her eyes.

I looked from her to the display of rocks and knew somehow before even asking. "These are parts of some of the rocks – the rocks that killed him?"

She nodded. "They're all around you. Some of them are in the walls. Some are in the products that I sell. Some of them form the foundation for this very building. I insisted on it. If Giles' demise stood to be the heart and soul of this store, then it's only fitting that it be part of the foundation, as well, don't you think?" She seemed to study us another moment or two, before continuing.

"A legacy," Chelsea explained, "is not always wrapped up in a land title, deed, or will. It isn't always something that can be evaluated with money or by any other materialistic means. For me, the legacy came in the form of those two words: 'More weight.' And those two words have allowed me to live my own life."

I nodded. The beauty of it all was even more apparent than when I first entered the establishment. I touched one of the smoothed stones reverently and understood the spirit with which it was all intended.

Under Suspicion

"Josie! Kelly! Did you girls take money out of my pocketbook?"

Our grandmother came into the back bedroom where my cousin Josie and I were playing with Barbie dolls. I was eight years old and already bored with summer vacation, just one week into the break. Josie and her younger brother Sam visited our grandparents every summer from Ohio.

I looked grandmother in the eye. She was angry; I could tell. She shook her pocketbook indignantly in our direction, yelling, "Well, I asked you a question! Did you take money out of my pocketbook?"

"No," I answered her quietly, ducking from the pocketbook that swung out in our direction.

"You better not be lying to me! I'll find out if you are!" She glared at us once more as she left the bedroom and slammed the door behind her.

Josie stifled a giggle until she heard grandmother griping her way back down the hall.

"Why is that funny?" I asked her.

"Why would we take money out of her purse?" Josie laughed outright. "If we want money, all we have to do is ask Grandpa. And if we were just gonna take money, there's plenty of it lying around all over the house."

Josie was right about both points. Our grandparents left money in odd spots all over the house. In trays on the dressers, in the medicine cabinets, in ash trays in the living room and family room. And Grandpa was an easy target when any of us wanted or needed some change. Still, if the money was missing....

"Are you sure you didn't take any money from her pocketbook?" I asked Josie, wondering if she would even tell me the truth if she had.

"No, Kelly! Geez!"

"Do you think Sam might have done it?"

She shook her head incredulously. "Please, Kell! Like Sam is that smart?!? I don't think so!"

For days, Grandmother watched every move we made. While we ate breakfast. While we made sandwiches for lunch. When we played outside in the backyard. When we sat on the glider on the front porch. When we walked around the house, left the room to go to the bathroom, or even when we got ready for bed. Constantly. Josie reached the point where she laughed out loud anytime she caught Grandmother watching, which only served to infuriate Grandmother more each time.

The next week, while helping Grandmother break beans from the garden, I needed to go to the bathroom. She looked from Josie and Sam to me and finally nodded her head, adding, "But don't take long! We need to finish these beans!"

I went inside and walked calmly to the bathroom, closing the door behind me. On the washer, I spotted Grandmother's pocketbook. I stared from the closed bathroom door to the washer and back again. With nimble fingers, I pulled the pocketbook towards me and pilfered through her overstuffed change purse. Coins threatened to spill out into the pocketbook, the clasp on the change purse barely closing over the multitude of nickels, dimes, and quarters inside. I deftly counted out $1.35 – the same amount I always took. Instead of putting it in my pocket, though, I carefully placed it inside the medicine cabinet, simultaneously proud of myself for having taken it and for having gotten away with it once again the day she interrogated Josie and me.

The Manor

At the party celebrating his 99th birthday, Varney Comer, a short and round, balding man, flat-footed with the assistance of his walker, hugged on all the women all day long, and pretended to hear what people said to him. The parishioners from the First Methodist Church came out in full force, laughing throughout the afternoon meal, smiling as Varney opened his gifts and visited with everyone.

Two of his twelve children (Louise and Shelby) were present; the others who lived close enough to come had likely not been invited. His son Dave had died two years earlier and the others had refused to play nice with each other ever since. *That's the saddest thing about someone dying,* Varney often thought. *The person dies, but too many times the family follows suit.* A daughter living out West had gotten angry because she wasn't consulted about whether or not she wanted to buy her deceased brother's house and it had all spiraled straight to hell from there. All of the kids would talk to Varney, but not necessarily to each other. Harsh words had been spoken; accusations had been made. They all lost Dave but, in the end, lost each other as well.

After the party, Louise and Shelby drove Varney back down the street of the small town to The Manor. The Manor. Varney couldn't decide whether to chuckle or scoff at the nickname for the facility where he lived. From bygone 1939, when he was still a young man of twenty-seven, he could hear Miss Scarlett saying, "Rhett, take me to 'The Manor,'" her glorious deep Southern accent deliciously silencing the "r" at the end of the word. It would have sounded like "manna," food from Heaven, but The Manor sure didn't offer that.

"Dad," his daughter Louise said loudly so that he could hear her, "Dad, I'm gonna put a piece of cake here in your little refrigerator, okay? If you want it later, you can have it then. Maybe you'll want it for dessert after supper tonight."

Varney nodded his head, agreeing with whatever Louise said, although, truth be told, he wasn't exactly sure what she had said. Something about he could eat the cake later, he thought.

Shelby asked something about how he liked his gifts. "I liked 'em right much," Varney answered simply. "It was awful nice of everyone to come and bring me stuff. I don't reckon I *needed* any of it, but it *was* right nice of 'em." Varney reached up and scratched his almost-bald head. Louise's daughter Jenny sometimes drove over from Wilkes County with her husband and two children to visit and would cut his hair with her clippers when she came. Everyone told him that he ought to go to the hairdresser that came to The Manor every Thursday, but Varney didn't much care for her demeanor. She wasn't very friendly, and Varney thought that $5 was a smart bit more than he ought to have to pay for getting the little bit of hair that he had left trimmed up a little. And that woman never made it look right. Jenny, though, well, Jenny would brush it and tenderly sweep it up so that it looked and felt the way that Varney reckoned it should. And Jenny did it for nothing but a hug and a kiss on the cheek. That suited Varney much better than pulling out a $5 bill from his worn-out leather wallet.

Louise and Shelby puttered around for a few minutes, trying to make sure that all was set right in the room that Varney currently occupied solitarily. He had been at The Manor almost two years and had outlasted three roommates – four, if you counted old Alvin Cox, whom Varney had threatened to suffocate in his sleep if Alvin didn't quit snoring at night. Poor Alvin had asked the nursing staff to be moved to another room that same week.

When Louise and Shelby finally took their leave, Varney sat there in the chair beside his hospital bed and closed his eyes. Sometimes it frightened him just how tired he could become from doing nothing but sitting. Up until two summers before, Varney had still lived independently, renting an upstairs apartment above one of the two convenience stores in town. The kids and grandkids worried about him because there were twenty-two steps to climb to get to the apartment. Jenny said that she didn't trust the steps, that they were too rickety. Eventually, the landlady had a new set built. Two weeks later, Varney fell going up them and chipped his hip bone.

He assured the kids that he had not fallen, but bruises on his back and legs begged to differ. The scariest part wasn't that he fell, Louise told him, but that he lay in his house for two solid days without being able to get to the phone to call for help. That is how he had come to live at The Manor. The doctors had forbidden him to live in the apartment, declaring that they would not clear him to go back to those living arrangements. He had gone to The Manor loudly and spitefully, crying like a baby, and begging Louise not to make him go. Varney had not wanted to go into a nursing home but, technically-speaking,

The Manor was not a "traditional" nursing home. The Manor served three separate purposes under one roof – a rehabilitation center affiliated with the county hospital, an assisted-living care facility, and a nursing home. Varney had started out in rehabilitation and had later moved into assisted-living; he hoped that he died before he had to move into the nursing home section.

Life here suited him well enough now, though. There were singings and storytelling and other activities like Bingo that he enjoyed. The dances were the best. But living here differed vastly from life before The Manor. Then, Varney cooked his own meals, usually frozen or canned vegetables from a little garden that he raised behind the convenience store, or from the gardens of friends, neighbors, and relatives. He canned the vegetables each summer, proudly showing off his beautiful treasures when folks stopped by to visit. Here, nothing tasted particularly fresh; in fact, nothing really *tasted* much at all. They couldn't cook with salt, added sugar, or spices much at all. "Dietary restrictions," he had been told by every nurse there, seeing as how Varney had complained at least once to each one about the blandness of the food. On days like today, he missed the food he had grown up on, animals hunted and trapped by his grandfather Jimmy, great-uncle Enoch, or himself. Jenny had asked him once what his favorite game was to eat. "I don't particularly have a favorite," he remembered telling her, "but I reckon I'm as fond of an apple-fed groundhog in Fall as anything else."

That made him recollect another question Jenny had asked that day. "How old were you when you killed your first deer?"

He replied, "Oh, I don't know exactly. I was a young man."

She had marveled at this answer. "A young man? Didn't Jimmy or Enoch teach you how to shoot deer when you were a kid?"

Now he was the one left in stupefied amazement. "Well, no. There weren't no deer here then."

Jenny, blown away, dumbly repeated, "What do you mean, there weren't any deer here then?"

Varney got a little agitated at having to explain something so simple to a woman in her mid-thirties. "I mean there weren't no deer here then! They'd all been hunted out and we didn't have none here until around 1938."

In retrospect, when he stopped to consider the deer population of Jenny's lifetime, he supposed that it might indeed seem peculiar to her to learn that deer, while now so overpopulated in the region, had in his earlier life been all but extinct. As a young man, a deer sighting was a rare thing, but now it was nothing to watch them nibble unafraid in people's gardens or dart out in front of motor vehicles on roads at all hours. He even knew folks who intentionally put out salt blocks in backyards for them.

Varney considered that he had actually lived many different lives in his one lifetime. He had been many things to many people: husband to three dearly-departed women, father to twelve children scattered all over, grandfather to eighteen, great-grandfather to thirteen, and great-great-grandfather to one. He had been hunter, trapper, fisherman, farmer, factory worker, sawmill employee, moonshiner, woodcarver, and more to support his family as best he could. He had raised hell, put people through hell, and reformed to fear hell, thanks to a good Methodist minister.

He remembered a time and place long ago when you didn't need to worry about the consequences of shooting any game you felt hungry for on any day, in any month, before established "seasons" prohibited such behavior. He remembered fishing nearby streams and creeks with primitive fishing gear, far unlike the fancy bobs and baits most of his sons and grandsons used. He remembered trapping minks and other now-seldom-seen animals when there were so many of them that you couldn't shake a stick at them. He remembered when people used every possible part of a killed animal because there weren't credit cards and fancy stores with factory-made-whatever for folks to run out and waste their money on.

He had lived through two World Wars and been spared service in each: the First because he was too young, the Second because he had a slew of kids, a pregnant wife, and never took the time nor interest to get personally involved. He reckoned it wasn't much of his affair what happened halfway around the world. He appreciated the local boys who had gone off to fight, but didn't envy them all of their medals and celebration upon returning home. He figured it was better not to have the nightmares and flashbacks that many of his boyhood friends brought back; he could walk through the dense forests of home without worrying that "the enemy" was hiding somewhere, waiting to send him to his Maker.

At the age of 99, Varney had never owned a motor vehicle, nor had a driver's license, but had walked probably every foot of land in a 75-mile radius. Birth certificates had not been required in Virginia until mid-June 1912, shortly after Varney's birth. He remembered when he turned sixty-five and it came time to sign up for Social Security. He had no documentation to prove his age and went back into the woods of Buck Mountain to the dilapidated home of his grandparents, weathered and worn, but still standing, searching through miscellaneous items left behind, just in case he could find something useful. He found the Family Bible, but no dates were recorded inside. When he went to the Social Security Office, he explained to a worker there that he had no birth certificate, no dates recorded in his Granny's Bible, no draft cards, no military service records, not even a driver's license. The man grinned, "Well, Varney, I know that my Daddy told me ya'll went to school together. Go down to the School Board and get 'em to write up something about your school records. That'll work as good as any of that other stuff!" How different from the present, when everything had its own set of paperwork, its own rules and restrictions, its own allowances and prohibitions!

Suddenly aware that he had nodded off to sleep, Varney jerked awake and sat up straight again in his chair. The smell of food wafted in from the hallway. A nurse brought in his evening tray and lifted the cover for him to see. Soup beans with no streaked bacon, greens without any vinegar, and cornbread not baked or caked with butter, or even margarine. That piece of cake sounded better and better to Varney.

Four Good Reasons

Reny Miller stood poised over her husband Elijah's slumped body, carefully gauging his intoxicated snoring and occasional muttering. He could wake from his stupor at any moment, or it may take hours for him to sleep it off. Carefully, Reny shifted her weight so that her good leg took more of the brunt of her frame than did the amputated limb perched on the cane-bottomed chair that she dragged along with her in order to make walking possible at all. The pistol felt heavy in her unwavering hand. Her finger rested securely against the trigger, waited patiently for the signal from her frantically-calculating mind.

A noise from the open door of the bedroom caught her attention, but she refused to be distracted. Someone was watching, she was certain. Who it was, was another matter. She doubted that it was one of the children. They had all been put down for a nap a short time ago and they probably would not have stopped short of where she stood, nor would they have remained so quiet.

"Reny," an older woman's voice finally spoke up, barely more than a whisper, with a strange sense of urgency and composure, "Reny, don't do it."

In an instant, Reny was able to snap off several unspoken questions. First was a poison-filled *Why the hell not?* Next, *Do you not think that he deserves it?* And then, *Is there a surer way for him to die and not plague me any longer?* All closely followed by, *How can you possibly defend him?* And finally an almost exasperated, *What else can I do?*

No words passed between the two women for several minutes, time seeming to stretch into eternity. Reny

retained her hawk-like position over Elijah, and Nannie
Lee, Elijah's mother, kept her post at the bedroom door.
Despite Nannie Lee's warning, Reny knew that the two
women were not exactly on opposite sides.

Nannie Lee's calm cadence again reached out to
Reny. "Reny, don't you do it. I ain't saying that he don't
deserve it. Truth is, I know that he deserves that and more.
I might be his mama, but I ain't fool enough to stand here
and try to defend him for the things he's done to you and
them babies sleeping in yon." She took a quick breath, and
then went on. "But Reny, them young'uns is four good
reasons why you can't do this."

Reny found her voice and finally replied, even
though her focus didn't stray from Elijah. "And you think
them young'uns are gonna have any easier a time of it with
him than I've had in these six years of marriage?" The
bitterness and pain in her voice came from the very core of
her being; her muscles were taut with remembering the
audacious atrocities that had befallen her since the day
she'd said, "I do."

Nannie Lee took a few careful steps forward. "I
pray to God that they will, Reny, but no, probably not. He's
enough like his old daddy that I'm afraid you're all in for
more heartache and hell. One thing's for sure, though, Reny
– they definitely won't fare any better *if you're not here* to
watch over them. *You* ain't Elijah Miller, and if you go
through with what you're fixed on doing here, you won't get
off as easy on it as Elijah did when he shot you."

At Elijah's sentencing for maliciously wounding his
wife a few months earlier, the judge had added that Elijah
couldn't very well be carted off to the state penitentiary

right then because his mother was consumed with cancer. If Elijah wasn't there, Reny couldn't take care of the dying woman because of her newly-acquired disability – rendered at the hands of Elijah, of course. Once Nannie Lee died, the judge promised that Elijah Miller would be taken to Richmond to begin serving his sentence. Most people didn't get that sort of luxury when sentenced.

Nannie Lee continued speaking softly to Reny. "And you know that I ain't long for this old world, Reny, so if you kill him and then I'm dead, who's gonna take care of them young'uns for us?" She paused, then asked again for emphasis, "Who, Reny? Tell me!" Nannie Lee gingerly touched her daughter-in-law's arm. Her voice was still very hushed, for Nannie Lee had no desire to rouse her drunken son, either. "Before you shoot him, you answer me that one question, girl! And if you can answer me that, I promise you that I will turn and walk out of this room and not speak a word against you in court if I live long enough to see your trial. 'Cos I know that *he deserves* to be killed. But we both know that your babies don't deserve what would lay in store for them if you do it."

Names flashed through Reny's mind like strikes of lightening in a summer storm. Names of family or neighbors who might be willing to take care of her four young children if she killed Elijah and was sent to prison. People who would treat them good after Nannie Lee finally succumbed to the cancer that had been ravaging her body for over a year.

Her own mama might, except for the fact that Reny's daddy hated Elijah Miller. Reny recalled going to her daddy once two years earlier, after Elijah had beaten her to within an inch of her life, begging him to help in some way. "Daddy, can't I please come home? Lije's got an awful temper and he's gonna end up killing me or one of the babies, I just know he is! Please, let me come home."

Her father had looked away from his daughter's face, adjusted his hat, and then spit tobacco juice sideways before looking back at her. "Reny, you can come home if you want to." He paused just long enough to see relief wash over Reny completely before adding, "But you can't bring Elijah Miller's bastards with you."

So that was the end of that. Saving herself would be easy. But if she left her children behind, they would surely be murdered in one of Elijah's fits of rage. Or, maybe even worse, they would be hauled off to the county orphanage where they might be in worse circumstances than if she just kept taking what Elijah dished out and stayed there to try to protect them as best as she could.

But how much more could she take? The cussings were nothing, really. And the beatings, well, she had about gotten used to them, too. Having a husband that gambled all of their money away if he felt like it and whored around whenever the notion struck him didn't break her heart like it used to, either. But when he was on a real rampage, like the one a few months back when he had shot her in the leg while she was still pregnant with the youngest of the four children – well, that night and all that it entailed was just sheer torture for Reny. There were no guarantees that Lije wouldn't do the same thing again, whether to her or the children. Lije already lit into the oldest child whenever the boy tried to take up for Reny, and Jason was only five years old. Could the child withstand another ten to twelve years of such abuse or worse until he left home to make it on his own? Could any of them handle whatever lay ahead?

If he could just be dead, she kept thinking. But she knew that Nannie Lee was right: if a jury found her guilty and they just might, because Elijah was well-connected throughout the county – then what would become of her children? She didn't care about what she might face herself; she was thoroughly convinced that it likely couldn't be any worse than half of the things that Elijah had already done to her.

Sometimes she wished that she had just had the foresight to get free of the situation the month after they married. On Christmas Day of that year, Elijah had gone on a turkey shoot with some friends and other local boys. Of course, they'd all been drinking all day long. The turkeys were probably safer than the people hunting them. And Elijah decided that he had had enough lip and attitude from his sister Beck's husband Frankie. After riding to his best friend Alley's house to get a gun that belonged to Alley, Elijah had ridden back through the meadows and woods near Beck and Frankie's house and claimed that he caught Frankie being mean to Beck. His claim of defense didn't stand up in court, but the coal company he worked for owned the law and all who worked within it in the rural county and arranged for a one-year sentence in the penitentiary even though it was easy to see the shooting was pre-meditated. Then, when Alley and Beck married just a few months later, it all looked even more suspicious. Reny and Elijah had been married less than one month when all of this transpired. She could have gone home then. She might have faced scorn, ridicule, and such from her father, but she would have been safe; there would have been no children to consider the futures of if she had just been that in-tune to the tumultuous marriage bed that she had made for herself.

She snapped back to the situation at-hand as Nannie Lee put her arms around her and pulled Reny's head onto her shoulder. Reny allowed Nannie Lee to do this, but still had the pistol trained on Elijah. "There ain't no one, is there, Nannie Lee?" Reny almost sobbed. "I can't think of a single person who would take my babies. But I still want him dead."

Nannie Lee stood back for a moment, looking from her daughter-in-law to her snookered son. If she didn't have cancer, there would be a way. She and Reny could stand together and do what needed to be done for those four precious grandchildren. Nannie Lee wasn't one for upholding murdering, but she understood Reny's position. How many times had she prayed for a way of escaping the hellacious scenarios with her own husband before he died? As she pondered the severe limitations of her own fragile life, she wondered how any of them could hope for a better future with the odds stacked against them so.

Reny lowered the weapon with an air of self-defeat, but shock coursed through her body as she realized that Nannie Lee had just reached over and taken the gun from her hand. Before she could even think of how to react, the whole house seemed to shake around her, as if a loud clap of thunder had landed four feet away from her in the middle of the bed where Elijah now lay bleeding. She looked in horror at Nannie Lee's distorted expression, then at Elijah's flailing figure finally coming to rest on their bed.

She gasped in surprise. Her mind could not at all wrap itself around what had just happened.

Nannie Lee held onto the gun and slowly walked to her son's still body. She checked for breathing, but found none. It was over then. That horrible part was over for all of them. What had been done could not be undone and she knew it full well. She couldn't explain her actions, not to Reny and not to herself, probably not even to the sheriff who would likely come calling later to see what all the commotion had been that the neighbors were all gossiping about. All she could do was quietly say to Reny, "Let them put me in jail, then. I'm almost dead anyway."

Learning to Drive

Mom's dad, Papaw Little, taught me to drive. I was sixteen and he was sixty-two. Anytime anyone in the family makes catty comments about my driving habits or skills, I always shoot back, "Well, *Papaw* taught me how to drive!"

Regardless of who is speaking, this statement is always answered with a snarky, "Yes, *I know!*"

No one else in the family would spend much time with me to help me learn how to drive. Mom got frustrated, furious, and flippant with me every time we went out to try. As a result, when it came time for me to drive with the driver's education instructor at the high school, I forfeited my turn. No one ever forfeited his or her turn to drive with Coach Peery! Without logging a certain amount of time out on the open road with him and two other students, one *could not* obtain a driver's license. "And why do you want to pass up your turn to drive with me?"

There was no point in lying about it. No point trying to craft some creative reason off the cuff and ride it out. I looked up into the face of this six-foot-something, sturdy-built baseball coach and practically whispered, "Because I don't know how to drive, sir."

He smiled. "Oh, no one really knows how to drive at your age. You've gotta get out there and do it in order to learn. The more you do it, the better you get."

"Well, sir, that's sorta the problem. No one in my family wants to be the one to teach me." This statement was verbatim what I had been told by both my mother and my stepfather, Tom.

Mr. Peery shook his head in disbelief. "If you let your turn go, you might not get another chance until sometime next semester. Didn't you just turn sixteen? You don't wanna be sixteen and not have your driver's license, do you?" he taunted.

The truth of the matter was that I really didn't care much one way or the other. I didn't like having people yelling at me and that was almost always the end result of a driving session with Mom. It seemed that I never did anything right when driving with her. It had gotten so bad one time that I pulled the car over to the right-hand shoulder, put it in park, and got out of the vehicle, leaving it running and my mother staring at me open-mouthed as I started walking towards home. When she found her voice, she yelled out the passenger window asking where I thought I was going. I answered, "Home. You can drive yourself there, 'cos I'm finished trying to learn how to do this!" I quit practicing. Until Mom talked Papaw into teaching me.

"Chrissle," Papaw addressed me using the shortened version of his pet name for me ("Chrissle-the-Gristle"). "Would you like for me to teach you how to drive?" For the longest time I looked at him, trying to decide if this was a joke or maybe some sort of mean trick. I finally shrugged my shoulders. I had already declined driving with Mr. Peery. "We're putting up hay this Saturday," he informed me. "Your first lesson will be up there. I'll be here by 10. Sharp. Understood?" I nodded my head in agreement and lived in anxiety for the remainder of the week.

Generally speaking, Papaw's temper landed much more securely on the "easygoing" side than Mom's. It took a lot to make him mad – but when you did, you better watch out!

Saturday morning, Papaw pulled up in his old beat-up red-and-white Ford pickup and blew the horn. I ran down the steps and out to the truck. He remained behind the steering wheel and I stood in front of the truck, a little confused. He called out the window, "Get in! We're gonna learn how to drive today!"

I walked to the truck and opened the passenger door. "Um, if I'm going to learn how to drive, shouldn't I be behind the wheel?"

"Not necessarily," he replied. "You can learn a whole lot about driving from watching someone else drive."

I couldn't help it; I rolled my eyes and sighed. So I really wouldn't be driving at all, I surmised. I would "observe" and "learn" from my observations. What a load of crap!

All day I sat on the passenger side, burning up in the last dog days of summer. Sweat ran down my face and neck. Even though the windows were down, no breezes floated about the entire morning and the heavy air seemed to blaze about us outside the truck. My stepfather and a couple of hired boys threw bales of hay up onto the truck from the early morning until the evening stretched out just before us. I squinted against the bright sun, wishing I had brought some paper or a book or could turn on the radio or do *something* to occupy my mind. *Lord, even country music would be better than this*!

The sweet smell of freshly-mown hay streamed through the open windows and I watched as grasshoppers sprang all around, looking for safety now that the tall stalks of grass had been cut down. The pretty purple clover that had been lost in a sea of green just a few days earlier lay beaten down amongst the grasses that would supply winter fodder for Tom's cows.

Papaw spent the day mostly talking to me about hayfields – about Granddaddy Vance's hayfields, his own hayfields, hayfields of friends and neighbors where he had worked when he was young. Once I allowed myself to listen to him without being disappointed or angry that my day had been "wasted" as a passenger, I found myself smiling, laughing, asking questions, and inserting my own opinions and ideas. I hung on every syllable uttered by his Northern and Southern accents, both spoken at once, a result of having lived so many years moving back and forth between Virginia and Michigan. Michigan, not because he wanted to be so far from home, but because that was where the better paying jobs were located then.

Papaw had sprinkled in questions about driving periodically, as though marking where the depths (or shallows) of my driving knowledge ended. He told me stories of his younger days and driving. "*Precautionary tales?*" I asked aloud, and he concurred.

After the next-to-last load of hay was unloaded, Papaw stood outside of the truck and drank a cupful of water from the Coleman thermos jug sitting on the floorboard at my feet. He wiped his brow and neck with the handkerchief from his back pocket. His eyes scanned the top of the hayfield, surveying how much work remained before sundown. "You reckon you're ready?"

My head twisted in his direction and my breath caught in my throat. "I, um, I – think so?"

He nodded and motioned for me to scoot over to the driver's side as he swung himself off the ground, up into the passenger side. "Now, you wanna be careful as you go up this way –" he started.

"Because there are four big groundhog holes," I finished. He nodded, smiling. He knew I had been listening and watching how he drove. I applied what I thought would be a little bit of pressure to the gas pedal and the tires spun on the cut hay as the truck struggled to gain traction under my sudden acceleration.

"Be careful how heavy you come down on the gas pedal. You ain't Mario Andretti, you know," he winked and chuckled a little.

"Sorry," I mumbled, steadying the speed.

At the top of the hill, Papaw said, "Whoa! I'm getting out here. Follow where I walk. I'm gonna lead you down through where these last few bales of hay are. When you get close to them, I want you to step on the brake and hold it there while I throw the hay up on the truck."

We wound our way down the hill, me pushing on the brake, and then easing the few feet to the next bale of hay. This repetitious go-and-stop continued for twenty minutes. Just when Papaw had gotten back in the truck, he spotted a few stray bales inadvertently left behind. "Pull across so I can get those, too." The angle at which I proceeded seemed a strain as I focused on the field, cautious. "Whoa!" he halted me again. "Pull to the upper side of this short row, and follow me down the hill."

The hay was piled high on the back of the old Ford. The back window was completely blocked and everything felt askew as I drove, each jolt seeming to shake the well-stacked hay just a tad too much for comfort. Suddenly, I realized that Papaw had told me to stop. When? Was it a half-second ago, a second, two seconds, longer? I had lost my focus and slammed my foot down on the brake, the truck skidding in the dew-dampened field as twilight continued its descent. The truck stopped with ample space from Papaw, but in the process, a dozen bales of hay toppled over the back of the cab and onto the hood and ground surrounding the truck.

With the truck securely stopped, I put it in park and closed my eyes, bracing myself for the yelling that I felt certain was coming my way. I realized how hard Papaw was working and scolded myself for causing him more work. I had started thinking about something other than what I had promised to focus on and…

I heard Papaw's breathing beside the open window and smelled his Avon Wild Country cologne commingled with the scents of a long day of hard, honest work, as he re-piled the runaway bales. When I felt his breath on my arm hanging out the window, I opened my eyes slowly, still expecting to be in trouble. "Now, Chrissle," he started slowly, and very solemnly, "you can't do what you just did."

"I didn't mean –"

"Hold on, and let me finish. You can't do what you just did because you will end up having a car wreck every

single time!" His voice continued to sound calm, not mean
or corrective, but concerned. "You got that? Don't EVER
jam on the brakes like that! You've gotta *ease* into it," he
instructed, stretching "ease" way out like fresh-pulled taffy
in a country store. He almost smiled, and then motioned for
me to pull ahead to the next bale.

After a couple of bales, he got out in front of me
again. I drove so cautiously now that I virtually crept along.
Only two bales remained. As I approached him, he called
out, "Whoa!" My right foot gingerly applied pressure to the
brake. "Whoa!" Slowly, slowly. "Don't EVER jam on the
brakes like that! You've gotta *ease* into it," I heard him
saying again in my head. "Whoa! Whoa! Whoa!!!" he
yelled out loudly. I looked up and saw his eyes wide open,
a look of abject horror on his face, waving frantically as the
truck finally came to a complete stop near him.

He strode to the open driver's side window and
demanded, "What the heck do you think you're doing? I
told you 'Whoa!' That means 'stop,' girl!"

Indignantly, I snapped back. "Hey, *you* were the one
who told me I had to 'ease' into it, not to ever *jam* on the
brakes!"

"Yeah, but you almost hit me!" he informed me.

"Oh, I had a good six inches before I would have
even touched you!" I retorted.

Neither of us looked away. Neither of us backed
down. Finally he laughed, shook his head, and waved me
off like a funny joke. "Let's get this last bale, and just do
what you know you're supposed to do." He paused for a
moment before continuing, "You did good today. Real

good. We'll start practicing on Baptist Valley Road tomorrow."

Does Your Papaw Love You?

It was early August 1982, just a few weeks before my eleventh birthday. My friend Debbie and I were spending the day together while she visited her grandparents for a couple of weeks, just like she did every summer. Debbie lived in Atlanta, a place I had never visited and didn't know much about, except that it was the capital of Georgia and a whole bunch of little kids had been kidnapped and killed there a couple of summers before. Even thought we didn't live anywhere near Atlanta, or even Georgia, Mamaw and Papaw kept an extra-close eye on my cousins and me the two summers those kids kept disappearing and then showing up dead. I worried about Debbie a lot since she did live close to where all those bad things happened; I was relieved that nothing bad like that happened to her in Atlanta.

Debbie's grandparents lived in a house in Baptist Valley, right beside the white farmhouse where my mamaw's parents lived before they died when I was seven years old. So, for as long as I could remember, Debbie and I had spent summers playing together in one of those two houses, or jumping across the dried-up creek bed that divided the two yards, or up in the pastures behind where my great-grandparents had lived. Even though no one in our family owned the white farmhouse anymore, we still sometimes played at Debbie's grandparents' house, although I preferred to have her come to where I lived so we could spend more time to ourselves and away from her grandparents. Her Mamaw Maxine was my mamaw's best friend. Her mom and my mom grew up together and sneaked cigarettes from adults and kept them in a secret hiding place behind my granny's house and smoked them when no grown-ups were watching. Both of our moms were divorced, too, so that was another thing that Debbie and I had in common that not a lot of other kids did. She had had a step-dad already, too, like me, and her mom was divorced from him now, just like my mom was divorced from my step-dad. I often wished that Debbie lived closer so we could do more together, but we made up for the distance during those couple of weeks each summer.

We competed over just about everything – grades, number of boyfriends, height, holding our breath under water. One Sunday morning, when we were eight, we even engaged in a singing competition at Yost Chapel Freewill Baptist Church. Debbie's mamaw sat in the pew behind my mamaw and papaw; her papaw didn't go to church. Debbie always wore a little denim skirt and t-shirt to church. I'd heard her mamaw complaining to my mamaw that Debbie's mom never sent any "*decent* church clothes" with Debbie for her visits, even though she knew that Maxine would take her to church while she visited. "Sheila never darkens a church door down there in Atlanta," she would say, "I reckon she's too busy with all those men she parades around in front of Debbie with to do something respectable like taking the child to church!" My dresses were home-made by mom, not store-bought, but they were always these frilly little things with bows and lace that made me itch. I always thought that Debbie's clothes looked a lot more comfortable, "decent" or not! Her pretty brown hair had these great curls, but she didn't have to sleep in those horrible pink sponge rollers like I did every Saturday night;

her hair was always curly. And not those old corkscrew curls that looked all fake like mine did, my own brown hair was so much longer than hers. Hers were just perfect – soft brown to match her eyes – and shiny, just like her perfect teeth and smile. Debbie and I sat together at church, giggling and flirting with a couple of the older Hankins boys a few rows back as Joe Baldwin, one of the church deacons, opened the worship service after Sunday school.

"Does anyone have a prayer request they'd like to share?" Brother Baldwin inquired.

Debbie's hand shot up and Brother Baldwin nodded to recognize her. "I'd like y'all to pray for my mommy, please. My mamaw says that she is lost and without the Lord." She seemed quite sincere in her proclamation, but I felt bad for her because I wasn't sure that she really knew what all of that meant, her not going to church much and all. I heard a couple of people snicker and saw Debbie's mamaw turn redder than a female red bird, as Jack Lane proclaimed, "Bless her, Lord Jesus!" I decided to let Debbie win this one, as my own mommy was saved and, even if she hadn't been, I knew better than to go telling it to everyone.

After prayer, Frances Colley came to the piano to lead our comely little church choir in a few hymns of fellowship. Of course Debbie and I made a charge for the piano so we could sing up there with the adults. Those beautiful hymns with words my head didn't always understand, but that somehow brought joy and peace to a part of me that I couldn't even explain. Without question, the song-singing was my favorite part of church. Even during the sermon, I often sat reading the words to the hymns, humming along in my head the ones I knew and wondering how the others might sound. *Love lifted me, love lifted me; when nothing else could help, love lifted me!* Or *What a friend we have in Jesus, all our sins and grieves to bear; what a privilege to carry everything to God in prayer.* And *Precious memories! How they linger, how they ever flood my soul; in the stillness of the midnight, precious, sacred scenes unfold!* I loved singing, with the choir or alone.

After the morning offering was collected by two of the Hankins boys, Brother Baldwin asked if anyone had a song to share. Well, God laid songs on *my* heart *every* Sunday, so I raised my hand to go first.

I made sure to walk up to the front of the church right by Crockett Harman. I don't know how old Crockett Harman was, but he seemed ancient to me. Thinning white hair adorned the top of his little round head. Glasses perched just a tad crooked on his sweet, clean-shaven face. He always wore a quiet smile and had a sense of peace about him even though he was what I heard another deacon call "old and afflicted." He wore the same plaid suit jacket every Sunday, usually a white button-up dress shirt, and darkish-colored pants. The left pant leg was pinned to the back of his pants, though, because he only had a right leg. I wondered what happened to his other leg, but I never asked him about it. He always offered a good, firm handshake to boys and girls alike, and made us feel included, not like we were in the way or unimportant. The thing that probably made Crockett Harman such a favorite with all the church kids, not just me, was that he always encouraged us to

participate in the service by rewarding anyone who sang
with his or her own pack of Juicy Fruit chewing gum.

I stood just a step to the left of the pulpit, and
proudly belted out "Touring That City," one of my favorite
church songs in the early 1970's. Upon finishing, I received
applause from the congregation and smiled. I walked
slowly to give Crockett Harman time to pull a pack of gum
from his jacket pocket. He handed it to me, patted me on
the back, and told me I'd done a good job. I thanked him
and returned to my seat beside Debbie. I unwrapped the
pack of gum as she watched and held it out to Debbie.
"Want a piece of my gum?"

She shook her head and informed me, "Nah, I'll just
get my own pack!"

And off she marched to the front of the church to
sing "Jesus Loves Me." The congregation clapped politely
and Debbie rushed over to Crockett Harman's side, holding
out her hand for her pack of gum. As she sat back down, I
rolled my eyes and asked, "'Jesus Loves Me?' Really? Was
that the best you could do, Debbie? We sang that before we
even started kindergarten!"

"Does anyone else have a song?" Brother Baldwin
asked, ready to turn over the service to Preacher Bostic.

"I do!" I proclaimed and jumped out of the seat,
going back up to sing another song. I gave "I'm Standing
on the Solid Rock" my best effort, even bowing to my
audience when it was over. There were a few chuckles, but
more clapping. Crockett Harman motioned me back over to
him for another pack of gum, an unexpected, but wonderful
surprise.

I hadn't even gotten to our seat when Debbie passed me in the aisle, going up to take a second turn herself. *Jesus loves the little children, all the children of the world...* I had to admit that it was a step up from "Jesus Loves Me," but it was still just a little chorus, not a full-fledged song like I had sung. I watched Crockett Harman fish another pack of gum from his jacket pocket and give it to Debbie with a bemused smile.

Preacher Bostic started to stand up from his seat on the front pew, but I spoke up. "Preacher Bostic, I've got another one, please." Our pastor grinned and motioned me to come on up, just about the same time my papaw looked over at me with a look that I knew meant I was pressing my luck. But the preacher had motioned me up, so I couldn't stop now. *Where could I go, oh where could I go? Seeking a refuge for my soul. Needing a friend to save me in the end. Where could I go but to the Lord?* The way Papaw was looking at me from his seat told me I probably should have gone nowhere and just stayed in my seat and not gone up front to sing a third song, but there was nothing I could do about it by then.

I also watched Debbie while singing that third song. She wriggled in the seat, nervously, and I knew that she was trying hard to come up with another song to sing. Since she didn't go to church back home in Atlanta, I realized that she probably didn't know many church songs, a fact that delighted me to no end in that moment, almost guaranteeing that this little contest was almost over and that I would be recognized as the winner. Poor old Crockett Harman had another pack of Juicy Fruit waiting as I left the stage and returned to my seat.

Debbie sat there contemplating deeply for just a couple of seconds. I grinned at her and said, "C'mon, Debbie! Just admit it – I won!" But before Brother Baldwin could even ask, Debbie called out, "Hey! I've got another song to sing, too!" By now, several church members were laughing, obviously having caught on to our little competition. Brother Baldwin turned away, trying to make his own laughter sound like a cough. And Crockett Harman had already begun fumbling around in his jacket pocket to find another pack of Juicy Fruit, making me wonder how in the world he kept all that gum from falling out all over the place!

At that precise moment, Debbie belted out robustly, *Delta Dawn, what's that flower you've got on? Could it be a faded rose from days gone by?*

About half of the church gasped, appalled by Tanya Tucker's country hit being sung in our Freewill Baptist midst. The other half of the congregation tried hard to control what might well have become an outbreak of cheers and jeers. I had already begun preparing another song in my head as Debbie came back with what surely must have been Crockett Harman's last pack of Juicy Fruit, but Papaw firmly put his arm on mine and informed me, "That'll be enough for today." And so our little contest ended in a tie, although I'm sure that Debbie's final song left far more of an impression that day than any of the songs I ever sang before that congregation!

****

"I asked you if your Papaw loves you," Debbie's voice brought me back to 1982, sounding somewhere between a plea and exasperation.

We were walking up the little dirt road from the yellow and white single-wide trailer where Mom and I lived to where a 3-foot-deep above-ground pool stood in the middle of the lower pasture of Mamaw and Papaw's farm. Mamaw and Papaw had bought it the previous summer to keep us grandkids out of their hair on hot summer days. My three cousins from Detroit, who came to visit every summer, were at the library with our aunt that day, though, so Debbie and I would have the pool all to ourselves for at least an hour or two.

"Well of course my papaw loves me!" I retorted indignantly.

She stopped for a moment and looked me in the eye. She looked scared. She seemed desperate to make me understand something that she wasn't giving words to. "No! I mean…" Her voice got hard, as though she could force me to understand the question in some way that I obviously failed to grasp it. "I mean – does your papaw *love* you?"

Her tone made me wary, putting me on high alert. I thought I was beginning to understand what she was really asking, but I didn't want it to be that kind of question. So I shrugged it off and simply responded, "Sure, my papaw loves me. We're buddies."

Her retaliating silence startled me. It wasn't in her nature not to shoot back with something like, "Well, my papaw loves *me* more" or "Me and my papaw are bigger buddies." The Debbie of three years earlier would never have left the matter unsettled like that. And that left me pretty unsettled.

We got to the pool, still lost in awkward silence. I removed a clothespin from the side of the pool and pulled back the sheet that covered the water to help keep out bugs and thirsty cows' tongues. I hosed off the bottom of the ladder, careful not to get any dirt in the pool and stood it straddling the side of the pool. I reached into the water for the long-handled net and skimmed the surface of the water, just to insure that there were no creepy-crawlies in there, dead or alive. The whole time, Debbie said absolutely nothing. She stood there with her eyes downward, as though there was a miniature carnival or something going on in the tall grass beside the pool.

I turned on my little portable radio to the local country station, "WTZE, in Tazewell, Virginia." David Frizzell proclaimed through song his plan to hire a wino to decorate his home, and then the Oak Ridge Boys crooned about "Bobbie Sue." Even though we splashed water at each other once or twice, nothing we tried did anything to lessen the hollowed-out emptiness that had settled between us over that grotesque, barely-spoken question that Debbie had asked what seemed like a lifetime ago.

Late-afternoon clouds rolled in just past 3:00. Lightning struck out on the horizon, a few ridges away, but blowing boldly in our direction. We climbed the ladder hastily, donning flip-flops, slipping and sliding as I tilted back the ladder to withdraw it from the water. I grappled with the sheet as the wind caught it like a rain-soaked sail rippling from a mast against a blackening sky. Thunder shook the ground as Debbie helped me clothespin the final portion of the sheet back to the side of the pool. We loped across the pasture, abandoning the dirt road for the most direct route back to the trailer, jumping across the little creek, rounding the corner of the fenced yard, and rushing through the gate that wouldn't lock just as the huge, hard drops started pounding our skin.

Debbie nearly tripped over the exposed roots where a maple tree once stood at the front end of the trailer as I skidded across the top step of the back porch and flung open the brown metal backdoor. Debbie reached down, removing her flip-flops, and then resumed running. She stopped inside the door on our multi-colored rag rug, mud sliding down her calves, discoloring her ankles. The raging wind slammed the door closed behind her and I could barely see her standing in the darkness of the hallway.

"Hold on, Debbie," I warned, "let me get some paper towels. Are you okay?"

"I broke my flip-flop," she muttered almost inaudibly, sounding like she might cry for its loss.

"Sorry about that," I answered. Then I asked again, "But are *you* okay?"

She might have nodded, but I couldn't be positive, the hall was so dark. I put down paper towels from the rug to the bathtub so she could walk into the bathroom a few feet away. Debbie walked delicately across them, like rocks across a creek where she might fall in. She climbed over the side of the tub. Sitting there, she wiped at the streaks of mud that caked her legs from her near-fall and running. I turned the water all the way over to cold and splashed water over Debbie's feet, flipping it gently onto her ankles, and then reached over to get a spot she had missed on the back of her left calf.

I hadn't even realized that I had touched her until I felt my friend flinch beneath my freezing fingertips. When I looked into her face, I witnessed something I had never seen there before. Fear. Out-and-out scared-ness. And I felt it breathing between us, smelled its repulsive, repugnant rankness, like the smell of the rotting baby calf struck dead by lightning last summer under a tree where it stood for shelter near the hayfield.

The brave little girl I had known all my life had trickled down the tub drain with the sobering streaks of mud. And in her place sat a stranger, someone unknown to me that day and forever after. "My papaw touches me," she trembled. "He loves me, so he touches me. Doesn't your papaw love you?" The urgency in her voice made me pity her, made me nauseous, made me sorry that I couldn't help her, frustrated that I didn't know how to help her in any way.

My own voice caught in my throat as the rain drummed against the tin roof of the trailer. I made myself look away and avoided her eyes as I whispered, "My papaw loves me too much to ever love me like that. I don't think that is love at all."

Debbie's fear and hurt blazed up into bitterness as she jumped up from the tub, wiping tears from her eyes, and setting her jaw hard as she glared at me. "It *is* love!" she insisted angrily as she stomped from the bathroom. At the end of the dark hallway, she hissed and threatened, "You better not tell nobody about my papaw and me, either!"

Without waiting for an answer, she retreated to the living room and I heard her calling her mamaw, saying yes, she was ready to go home.

I didn't leave the bathroom. I cleaned up the paper towels and threw them in the little bathroom trash can. I ran water in the tub, scalding hot this time. Long after every trace of dirt dissipated down the drain, I kept the water flowing, taking out the bleach from under the sink and pouring the remainder of the jug on every possible part of the bathtub, desperate attempts of disinfecting something that I could not even see. The harsh smell of bleach filled my nostrils like the nauseating stench of reality that had emptied out my soul in those brief moments. I heard the front screen door slam and Debbie left without saying good-bye.

I sat there in stilted silence, sobbing uncontrollably. Why couldn't I talk to her? Why couldn't I tell her? Her papaw had tried to love me, too.

Part II

Poetry: Lyrics and Verse

I Didn't Get Anything of Granny's

I didn't get anything of Granny's
when she passed in '78.

And once her daughters
feuded and fought
when Granddaddy died
the next year
(refusing to leave a proper will
because they were casting lots
for all belongings
days before he died),
there wasn't much of anything left
and I was only eight,
so what could I have done
and would I have even known
of anything to ask for?

The home place
was sold in no time flat
by the antique-hound sister:
lots of other people
got Granny's stuff – not me.

The youngest sister
seemed to get things
of deeper meaning,
not just materialistic value,
and shared them with her children;
her oldest daughter

got Granny's rosebush,
or at least enough of it
that part of Granny's rosebush
now grows in her backyard.

Granny's rosebush,
the one that grew outside
the parlor's front-view window,
far away from windows that opened
so she could enjoy its beauty
with the safety and comfort
of the glass
between it and her,
because her asthma prohibited
inhaling its lovely fragrance directly –
so she sat sometimes and just stared at it,
telling us that it was beautiful
just the way it was,
even though she couldn't smell it.

No, I didn't get anything of Granny's,
nothing like land, antiques, rosebushes...

But I did get her middle name:
Mom named me Irene for Granny;
Irene, meaning peace.
My Granny gave me peace.

I guess that's something, after all.

Road Trip Graffiti

Welcome home 278th!
I ♥ U Kim.
Come home soon.

Jason sux.
For a good time call –
Go to hell, fag!
Liz is easy.

God is watching us.
Pray for peace
          Or die trying.
Jesus loves you.

Kill your TV!
Now's the time.
Save the environment –
          Wear a fur.

Do you know where you are?
Hey, watch this!
Almost home.
Hell, yeah!

Speaking in Tongues

I remember old-time church meetings,
pleasant dinners on the ground.
Preaching would last for hours.
Hallelujahs kept resounding,
shouting, singing, praises ringing.
Then the Spirit would come descending,
and people would utter
indecipherable phrases,
almost chanting while they were praising.
Then they'd start dancing,
violent flat-footing
there at the altar,
hands raised high,
outstretched toward heaven,
till the Spirit slayed them all.

Hillbillies

Betty's father asked
with his Lake Superior accent
(more like warned her
in the clothing of a question),
"See those boys?
They're hillbillies,
and you best leave them alone!
Bring one home
and I will kill you,
not just you, but both of you!
Damned old hillbillies,
good for nothing,"
the father spat as they drove by.

And Bill had sat there,
with his brother Arthur,
never knowing, nor suspecting
that fate was fleeting,
time was tempting,
and God was laughing almost aloud.
Just fixing a tire
on their old Chevy,
the one that carried them there
from old Virginnie,
and while he was fixing,
she was fixing
her eyes on him,
her own hillbilly.

Ice Cream Truck

Summertime, when I was a kid,
an ice cream truck sometimes came down
Baptist Valley, mostly for the instant profits
made off the kids in the trailer parks.
But Mamaw and Papaw lived in
a yellow double-wide, way up on a hill,
and us grandkids could hear the music,
like a carnival barker beckoning,
a good five minutes
before it would pass the turn-in
to the little dirt road
that no ice cream truck would ever take.
Like starving vultures, the five of us
would descend on Papaw, who told us,
"Go ask your Mamaw,"
so we would elect Melenia,
the fastest runner of the five,
and she would take off
sprinting for the main road
while we helped Mamaw fish change
from her pocketbook,
then took off running as hard as we could
for the ice cream truck that would be waiting
for the "other four kids with money"
that Melenia had promised were coming.

Childhood Sunday Mornings

Childhood Sunday mornings,
I awoke to the smells of breakfast:
bacon and biscuits and fresh-brewed coffee,
sometimes, fresh-made French toast with syrup;
or, if Papaw was left in charge, fried hotdogs,
cut long-ways, and eaten right out of the skillet.

The double-wide came to life
with the bustling and beautification
of three women on a mission
to be pleasing before God (and neighbors),
and Papaw and me just trying our best
to stay out of those paths of intensity.

Mom unrolled those horrid pink sponge curlers,
my long, brown hair hanging in corkscrew curls,
so my hair would look like
Nellie Olson's on Little House,
then Mom would put me in some frilly dress
to complete my utter agony.

To pass time, I watched local on-air preachers
Brother Leonard Repass out of Bluefield,
and Jack Harmon, the host of Huff-Cook Funeral Home's
"Gospel Sing," on WCYB in Bristol,
and Oral Roberts, who always promised,
"Something good is going to happen to you!"

Mamaw would emerge from the bathroom,
a cloud of Aqua Net not far behind;
while Mom washed her face with Noxzema,
and then smoothed on her Cover Girl foundation;
and my aunt Susan, in her teenage angst,
pretending not to care about any of the ritual.

Then there was Papaw and me, looking at the clock
on the wall above the buck stove,
yelling, "Hurry up, women! It's time to go!"

Crying

I don't shed tears
that cascade gently
down my cheeks.
(How I wish!)
No,
I cry
noisy,
gulping,
ugly,
unpleasant
sobs
that give me a headache
and cause the snot
to run out of my nose.
There is nothing delicate
about the way in which
I purge
my soul of
its barest emotions.

The Saddest Obituary

CORBIN –
Randall "Randy" Pruett, 46.
No funeral service
or visitation;
the family
has chosen
cremation.
Corbin Funeral Home
in charge
of arrangements.

No mention of the fact
that he was a son
of two living souls;
no mention of the fact
that he was a father,
and a grandfather;
no mention of the fact
that his smile was amazing,
that his laugh was contagious,
that he loved music
and strummed the guitar
as a teenager;
no mention of the fact
that he tolerated
me as a kid
who followed along
behind him
like he was the coolest person
to ever walk the earth.

Winter Rains

Swollen ditches
engorged with water,
racing on
to unseen endings,
spill onto highways
not retreating,
unrelenting
as they charge
across pastures
of huddled livestock
looking on
as puddles widen,
becoming streams
that go from pools
to more-defined inlets,
into creek beds
long-forgotten
and trampled under
by man and time.
Still, the land
recalls those pathways
and commands the chaos
in the right directions
because the land
cannot forget,
and does not disown
what rightfully belongs,
no matter what
man puts asunder.

Freedom

Freedom feels like Friday
after a high school football game,
that phase of the night
when you fly with your friends,
coursing down country roads
like the blood boiling in your teen-aged veins,
blowing down backroads
with the windows down,
the radio reverberating,
and the soundtrack of
youth-approved abandon
making everything worthwhile.

Dog Days and Dragonflies

On hot summer days
Mamaw made us play outside
for as long as humanly possible,
so we weren't in her hair
and didn't mess up
her immaculate house.

I hated playing outside.
Four cousins, three from Detroit
just in for the summer,
every summer, when we were kids,
and me, the naïve native
of small-town America.

No one wanted us underfoot,
so we played
in the fields, in the creeks,
in the woods, in the barn loft,
and sometimes in the waterhole
that my uncle made with the tractor.

Before dumping into the waterhole,
cold water from the spring
back up on the hill a ways
continuously flowed
through the meandering creek,
with a fence down the field that kept
Mamaw's and Aunt Betty's bulls apart,
and kept Mamaw and her sister Betty

from locking horns, too.

I shiver when I remember
how breathtakingly cool
the fresh spring water felt
when we first climbed in,
then acclimating there
against sweltering Dog Days,
squishing mud up between our toes
and laughing out loud,
not-so-secretly hoping
that it was mud, and not cow manure.

Watching cows grazing on Betty's side,
and sometimes on Mamaw's,
hearing the sounds of the farm equipment
up in the hay field, where men and boys
worked harder than we could yet,
ducking for cover from occasional hornets,
simultaneously mesmerized and terrorized
by dragonflies hovering
around our make-shift pool.
Splashing and soaking up
all that life had to offer
in a place with little entertainment,
save what you could make on your own.

Priest of Nothing

Here I sit, a priest of nothing –
A cryer in the night –
An outcast from that which I create –
A loser of my own fight.
One who has a place in nothingness,
A counsel for broken hearts,
A matchmaker of my own desires
Who catches the falling parts.
One who worships friendship
And all the lies it holds;
A bather in the moonlight
Who suffers desert colds.
A giver who takes everything
For the mere idea of giving,
A lover who dies for anyone
So that others may go on living.
A dreamer who faces the reality
Of fatalistic dreams,
The fool who goes on hoping
For brighter human themes....
The perfect friend of toleration,
A fool; a pal; I'm all
To anyone who feels the need;
I answer any call.
And answer in the end, myself
The coldest judge to face,
Demanding an end to everything
– This supercilious race.
A cryer in the night; lone justice exists as real as do I;

A poet, priest of nothing, who writes as the world goes by.

Leah's Lullaby
(Song Lyrics)

Life is not a fairy tale –
it isn't heaven, it isn't hell,
sometimes it's good, sometimes it's well,
not quite like we planned.
It's more than just us growing old,
it's more than doing just what we're told –
the mysteries that we unfold
and try to understand.

The most that we can hope for is each day
to show someone we care for them in our own special way.

Close your eyes and go to sleep;
there's just one promise that you should keep:
what you sow is what you reap,
so do the best you can.

Summer days now in the past,
firefly glimmers that never last –
the memories that they all cast
bring to mind a smile.
Holding hands in August's rain,
comforting in times of pain,
relationships that we sustain
make it all worthwhile.

It's never quite as bad as we perceive,
almost as good as we ourselves will let ourselves believe.

Close your eyes and go to sleep;
there's just one promise that you should keep:
what you sow is what you reap,
so do the best you can.

What you sow is what you reap,
so do the best you can.

Cold

Winter mornings
my mother woke up early
to start breakfast,
spreading out butter
on slices of light bread,
placing them on an old
warped cookie sheet
that wobbled in the oven,
turning the oven setting to broil,
leaving the oven door open
to heat the room as well as the toast,
making buttery lakes of goodness
on the side that faced up.
Then she would call me
from the bedroom that we shared
and I sleepily shivered
past quilts hung in
every single doorway
to keep heat in our room
where a little heater stood.
I bathed quickly
in lukewarm water
that she ran from the kitchen sink
into a bedpan,
because the shower was downstairs
and there were no steps inside
and snow was falling
or water was freezing,
and she dreaded the cold
as much as I did.

And as we left for school and work,
she checked the heater
and the oven,
made sure the quilts
were nailed securely to doorframes,
and as we sat in the green Ford pick-up,
rubbing our hands together,
waiting for the cab to heat up
and praying the ice on the windows
would just melt,
she told me,
"Come payday,
we'll get more coal."

My Mother

My mother is a worker
and has been for as long as I've known her,
never one to take hand-outs:
when down-and-out, get up and go,
don't sit down and give up;
don't air any dirty laundry,
it's nobody's business but our own,
because God already knows what we need.

She never signed up for welfare,
when raising me on her own,
sporadic child support payments,
working a job that killed her feet,
made it tougher on varicose veins,
but somehow making sure
that what we had sufficed,
met our needs if not our wants.
Like the Christmas I wanted an Atari,
but knew there was no money,
and went back to school to learn
that I was one of the very few
kids not playing Pac-Man day and night,
and I went home and told her,
"Even the *welfare kids* got Ataris!"
And she answered simply, "Well, *we're* not welfare kids!"

Years later, she is disabled;
yet she works at what she can, when she can.
I ask what she's doing this weekend,
I might come visit if the weather holds,

and she tells me that she's cooking on Friday,
then going out to read the Bible
to old Ms. Newman, who just turned 98,
then on Saturday, she and cousin Fanny
are taking food "to the little people,"
the ones no churches could take time for,
and God told her that they were hers,
to serve them in His name,
so she cooks for them, the elderly and alone,
and shares good news and God's love,
until mid-afternoon each Saturday,
each week that weather permits.

I wonder if I've ever told her
how I admire these "little things,"
as she calls them – these little things
that mean so very much to so many others –
shut-ins and old folks and the nursing homes, too….
Whether it's fresh fruit, or cornbread,
or just taking the time to visit,
she shares her generosity, an infectious laugh,
and would give you the shirt off her back
if people would not talk about her
for not wearing one in public.

Wrapping Meat

Butchering beefs came early
in fall, the air not yet crisp
or coolish, sent to Lambert's
Packing House for the kill,
then returned three days later
in blood-stained cardboard boxes
lined with white freezer paper,
saturated with the rawness
of winter's eatings.
Granny, Mamaw, and Mom
making up an assembly line,
laboring at length over T-bones
and round steaks, sirloins and butt
roasts, and hamburger, so much
hamburger to be patted, then stacked,
freezer paper inserted between
each patty, freezer paper torn
big enough for four patties flat,
then four patties tall, and then
wrapped up within more white
freezer paper and identified with
magic marker, the date and package
contents, the colors bleeding into the paper
in benzene-emboldened script,
unmistakable marker smell permeating
the entire kitchen while these women,
my foremothers, laughed hard but
worked harder, telling tales, giving gossip,
sharing wisdom, making memories.

I hovered near, or beneath the table,
trying to be included, but not be
under foot, listening and loving,
the benzene in the markers
marking the packages of meat, but also
marking me and those childhood days
in ways I still can see.

Come Home, My Cousins, Come Home

Come home, my cousins, come home!
From your places in the cities
and the suburbs they have spawned,
come home to the country,
to the mountains and ridges,
to the creek banks and pastures,
and the farmland that's left here.

Come home to the places
that your parents once knew:
Dry Fork, Thompson Valley,
Amonate, and Bishop,
Baptist Valley, and Dix Creek,
Mundytown, Adria,
and Stoney Ridge, too.

Come home to the places
that your grandparents called home:
Horse Creek, Hurricane,
White Top, Nella, Windfall,
Lansing, and Helton, and Piney Creek,
Walnut Hill, Chestnut Hill,
West Jefferson, too.

Come home, my cousins, come home:
your roots and your branches
can stretch and grow here,
your family is waiting,
and the memories of generations

who paid prices and sacrificed,
and made your roads ready,
so that you could go where you needed to
to make your own ways.

Crazy

Uncle Jimmy got sick
last winter, found himself
somewhere between
"just living" and "not,"
and started thinking
about things that

have troubled him long
decades, not just the
ghosts from Vietnam,
but perceived
atrocities from much
closer: "I helped move

people from graves at
the state mental
hospital," he whispers,
his eyes seeing a
time when money
was tight. "Unmarked

graves to unmarked
graves, like they weren't
nothing but garbage
moved from one dump
to another one, like
they weren't even important

enough that someone,
someday, might come
looking, might start
wondering, like they
weren't even people
in the first place." His

head shakes, he stares down
the past, heart burdened. "For
a little money," he feels
the heaviness of Judas'
coin collection. "Those
were people, no matter
what the state thought
they was. I think now,
we're the ones who were crazy."

About the Author:
Chrissie Anderson Peters grew up in Tazewell, Virginia. She graduated from Tazewell High School, and completed her BA in English/Education from Emory & Henry College. She received her Masters in Information Sciences from the University of Tennessee. She currently works as a librarian at Northeast State Community College in Blountville, Tennessee. She resides in Bristol, Tennessee, with her husband Russell and their feline children. For more information, check out her website, www.ChrissieAndersonPeters.com, or email her at TheWriteWayToGo@gmail.com.

About the Book Cover Artist:
Beth Jorgensen is a mixed media artist in Phoenix who specializes in oil painting. Her predominant style is realism, particularly pieces that focus on human interaction while employing subtle humor. Her current major body of work is an in-progress series of large-scale oil paintings that feature people in awkward, ironic and/or humorous situations while inside elevators. In addition to her realistic pieces, Beth also experiments in the realm of abstract painting, in which she plays mostly with color and texture. Having drawn ever since she remembers being able to hold a pencil, Beth relocated from southwestern Virginia to Tempe, Arizona, after high school to attend Collins College in 1995 for graphic design. Later in 2003, she went back to school at Arizona State University to obtain her Bachelor of Fine Arts degree (graduating in 2007). While Beth is a painter above all else, she is comfortable working in any medium and style. Her current elevator series can be viewed online at http://home.takethestairs.net, and she can be contacted about her work by email: beth@takethestairs.net.

Made in the USA
Charleston, SC
15 November 2012